D1590677

To Doris,

with God's blessings

THE GOOD SOLDIER
Running on the Road of Hope

Dr. Elie Hasbani

WESTBOW
PRESS
A DIVISION OF THOMAS NELSON

WestBow Press books may be ordered through booksellers or by contacting:

WestBow Press
A Division of Thomas Nelson
1663 Liberty Drive
Bloomington, IN 47403
www.westbowpress.com
1-(866) 928-1240

ISBN: 978-1-4497-2799-4 (sc)

Library of Congress Control Number: 2011917913

Printed in the United States of America

WestBow Press rev. date: 10/20/2011

Dedication

I dedicate the Good Soldier to my wonderful family, particularly to my understanding and patient wife. I also dedicate my book to the hopeless in the world and those who search for peace. I also appreciate all friends who supported me through the process.

CONTENTS

Prologue

The beautiful land of Lebanon is my home by birth. I am my parents' first child, a son. And I was raised a Christian in the faith and practices of the Roman Catholic Church. These circumstances of birth form the foundation of my earthly identity as an Arab Christian. They represent the personal and cultural cornerstones for my life's ambitions and allegiances. At least they did until my identity, my ambitions, and my allegiances were all confronted by the person and kingdom of the Lord Jesus Christ. And that has been the story of my life, a story of the ongoing transformation brought about by the loss of all those self-identifiers that seemed so important to me as I was growing up.

The pruning work of the heavenly vinedresser began to cut painfully at those fruitless branches of my life. A patriotic love for my earthly homeland was refined in the heat of the Middle East wars between Muslims and Jews. The selfish privilege and burdensome requirements for a first-born son were challenged by personal failures and by the trials on battlefields in south Lebanon. And the lifeless support of a religious faith based on mere culture and tradition proved to be ineffective and meaningless as I came to maturity in a carnal and hate-filled military environment.

But at last, all of the human failures compounded by the difficulties of historical circumstances came to a head when a landmine exploded beneath me. In that moment my life was changed forever as I called out to Jesus and yielded to His lordship and His kingdom. The loss of my left leg was the catalyst experience that God used to turn my life in a whole new direction. My former allegiances as a soldier fighting in a physical battle were replaced by a good soldier fight in a spiritual battle for Jesus Christ (2 Timothy 2:1-4). Old ambitions yielded to seeking out God's purposes for my life. And my earthly identity began a renewal in the life of God. Beyond the dismembering tragedy, the heavenly Father was teaching me how to fight the good fight and to shine like a star to the nations.

My desire and prayer as you read my story is that your faith would be increased to trust that God is well able not only to find you and redeem you from your own personal predicaments, but that he is wholly adequate to deal with all of the problems and crises facing the world in which we now live. With God, nothing is impossible!

PART I
MY ROOTS

Chapter 1
Lebanon the Beautiful

God created the nations with the intention that each should
seek him and find him. Varied cultures have risen on the
face of the earth. Mine was in the ancient land of Phoenicia
which today is called Lebanon. It is my home by birth.

Wadee' El Safi, a popular Lebanese singer, gives us the lyrics of a familiar ballad extolling Lebanon's virtues. This awkward translation suggests the pride and honor held by the people of the land for their home, their traditions, and their history.

> Lebanon is a piece of heaven on earth.
> It is a beautiful painting by God.
> We are very hospitable
> And welcoming to our guests.
> Yet our swords are ready to kill our foes.
> O Lebanon, peace of heaven,
> Ours lips always lift you in our prayers.

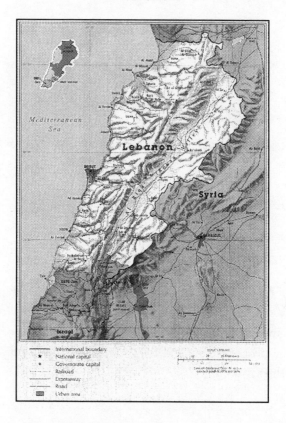

"Lebanon during the civil war".

I love my native homeland. The land is one of beautiful terrain and pleasant climate. Its culture is characterized by a courtesy and hospitality demonstrated in the relaxed lifestyle of its people. And in many ways its citizens have a noble ancient history coupled with a unique modern perspective. The Bible speaks of the beauty and bounty of Lebanon. When pleading with God for a chance to enter the Promised Land, Moses mentioned Lebanon by name as part of the "good land" he longed to see on the other side of the Jordan River. King David's desire to build God's temple in Jerusalem included plans to obtain that exceptional and fragrant wood from cedar trees growing on the slopes of Lebanon's mountains. King Solomon sought the goodness of God on his own land by saying, "Let grain abound throughout the land; … Let its fruit flourish like Lebanon." (Psalm 72:16 NIV) And at least one Old Testament prophet saw that Lebanon and her people would also experience the blessing of spiritual and physical healing as a part of the fruitfulness of Messiah's coming kingdom (Isaiah 29:17ff). In his passion for all peoples, God has greatly blessed and dearly loved my native land. And so do I.

Lebanon is a small country at the eastern end of the Mediterranean Sea. It is surrounded by Syria on the north and the east. Israel is on her southern border. The Lebanon Mountains run north and south through the land leaving a very narrow strip of pleasant coastal plain on the west. The Anti-Lebanon Mountains are to the east and run parallel to the Lebanon Mountains, creating the Bekaa Valley. The ancient cedars of Lebanon still grow on the mountain heights. Lebanon's capital city of Beirut has a commanding view of the sea and has long been considered a financial and educational center, as well as a vacation destination for much of the world. The pleasant climate, historical and archaeological sites make it attractive for tourists. It is no wonder Lebanon has been called the Switzerland and Beirut the Paris of the Middle East. I grew up being proud of my heritage and loving the land into which I had been born.

As a young child, I learned to love the beautiful countryside and refreshing air of the mountains. Every spring when the school year had ended in Beirut, our family would pack up and make the trip south and east to spend the summer months in our parents' home village in the mountains. To get to Deir Mimas, we would rent a taxi and make the daylong journey, first traveling south past Saida (Biblical Sidon) and then east through Nabatiyeh, which is surrounded by the beautiful mountains of Lebanon. After the long day of travel, we would at last arrive at the village of Deir Mimas facing Mount Hermon, its peak still covered in snow. The village is situated on the Litani River at an elevation of about 2500 feet above sea level. It is surrounded by two huge mountains and a stone fortress built around the 12th Century. The countryside is covered with thousands of olive trees, watered by more than sixty springs, making the area famous for its quality olive oil.

My grandfather was a shepherd. I remember the year when I was old enough to be allowed to walk with him as he led the sheep to pasture. Early in the morning I watched as my grandfather put on the special boots and clothing that protected him from the rough ground he would be crossing. He also packed his lunch in a special bag called a *ziwwadi*, a type of cloth in which the food is wrapped and then tied at the top to hang from a wooden rod. He had dogs that would accompany him to help guide and protect the flock. I had dreamed of the day my grandfather would take me with him for many years and now it had come. We set out in the dark morning hours. I watched him as he directed the flock and saw him throw a cautionary stone if a sheep went astray. He hung bells on some of the strongest sheep so the others would follow their lead just as they in turn followed my grandfather's lead. He knew each lamb, naming them all; at least three hundred of them. Some had names such as 'Strong' or 'Weak.' I noticed that one sheep had a ring around his neck with bells attached to it. I asked my grandfather about him. "This one is very strong and he knows me well. The other sheep are afraid of him and will follow him." I was amazed when my grandfather would say one little word and the entire flock would obey. He carried a special rod, the shepherd's staff, using it to help him as he walked and to guide his sheep. He would tap a sheep on its horns to guide it; and he would rest on the edge of the stick when he was tired.

Because my father was an officer in the Lebanese army, we lived in an apartment complex for military personnel in Beirut during the school year. There I became familiar with the cosmopolitan dimensions of twentieth century Lebanon. My experience as a child was neither parochial nor clannish. I grew up being well aware of the wider world around me, sensitive to the cultures and historical perspectives of both the East and the West. In school, we were taught a second language such as French or English. We were given every opportunity for careers appropriate to the modern world. It was quite natural under these circumstances for me to want to build a life on the normal human longings for abundance and security. It was, however, the pastoral life of the Lebanese people in the countryside that added a sense of peace and well-being to my young life

The culture and customs of Lebanon reflect the casual and hospitable nature of its people. For the Lebanese, there is always time to socialize and share refreshments. Such friendship and courtesy were not limited to a particular social status or religious group. I remember the people of

Lebanon showing gracious respect for other backgrounds and religions. It was our national way of life. The military apartments we called home in Beirut were a melting pot of religions and ethnic customs. The Muslims and the Christians lived together in a community of friendship and love. Everyone knew each other in our neighborhood, their families, and their backgrounds. Each morning, after the children were sent off to their schools, mothers would meet for coffee at various houses to talk and enjoy a relaxing time together before each one would go back to their daily chores at home. They called this time *subhieh*. Everything was shared among family and friends. People were there for you if you needed help. It was said, "A close neighbor is better than a distant brother" and I saw that lived out everyday.

The parking lots of the buildings were turned into playgrounds for all the kids in the neighborhood. When the school day was over, we spent most of our time in these playgrounds. I played soccer with the other boys and my sisters usually spent their time jumping played jump rope with the girls. Sometimes we didn't have a ball to play with so we would use an empty bottle or anything that looked slightly round. We never had a basketball hoop so we would use a broken wooden chair on a pole and aim the 'basketball' at the hole of a broken seat. We had great fun despite the less than professional equipment. As with all children, fights would sometimes break out during the games and some of the kids would throw stones in anger. I occasionally got hit in the head and would run home crying and screaming to my mother. She would put ice on my head and rubbed coffee grounds into the wound to stop the bleeding and life went on.

Coffee and tea are the most popular social drinks in the Arab world. They are served to visitors at home and in work places. The choice between coffee and tea is partly a matter of local custom and supply and partly a matter of personal taste. Among Christians, coffee is commonly called Turkish coffee. It is a strong drink made from very finely ground, dark beans, boiled in a little pot, and often served in demitasse cups or glasses. In the evenings, families would visit with each other, talking over coffee, playing cards, or watching television, if there was one in the home. The children would play together apart from the adults. This time was called *sahriya*. I remember times when we would have people in our home and they would stay very late. If people didn't come to us, we would be at their home doing exactly the same thing!

Deir Mimas my home town (Elie's house circled)

The traditional Lebanese hospitality was quaintly evident in the countryside of our native village, Deir Mimas. Whenever we would visit, our arrival there was a village-wide event of joyous celebration. We would greet each other with phrases such as "Peace be with you" or "God be with you" or *"Yaatik al-aafief,"* meaning "God give you strength." Cultural custom considered it rude not to say, "Good morning" or "Good evening" or a simple "Hello" to someone you know, even if you knew the person only casually. When you entered a room, you were to greet all the people who were already there, whether you knew them or not. Hospitality is a highly prized cultural practice. A visit to relatives or friends in their home or workplace would almost always include at least something to drink. If you were invited to a meal, lots of food should be expected. The hosts would go out of their way to serve you the most lavish meal they could. Food would be piled on your plate and insist that you eat more! When you had enough to eat say, *"Al-hambo-lillah"* ("Praise God" or "Thank God"). This is one of the most widely used phrases in the Arab world by people of all religious backgrounds.

Weddings are an especially joyous time for a community. It was the custom in our village to start inviting all the village families to the wedding one month before the actual date. Friends and relatives of the bride and groom would go around two by two or three by three, carrying flowers in their hands and knocking on the doors of all the houses, and saying, *"Inshallah Al-Afrah Doum Bidiyarkon"* (God keep joy in your house); you are invited to the wedding of so and so." The second part of the invitation was to distribute a wedding card to each family. The finally, the parents of the bride or the groom would deliver personal invitations. Very formal visits were made to special people and relatives in order to invite them personally. Parties would start two weeks before the wedding. Each night the young men and women would meet in different homes to celebrate. The main party was the night prior to the wedding day. All the guests of the wedding would attend with the whole family and have dinner prepared by the women in the village. On this occasion, *arak* is served. Arak is a traditional Lebanese drink consisting of fermented grapes and anis. The arak is served in special glass jars called *ibreek* which are usually only used for drinking water. This *ibreek* is a type of pitcher with a handle and a spout. The intention is to pour the arak into glasses from the spout, but often the *ibreek* is passed around to the guests who take a drink by pouring directly from the spout into their mouths and then pass it on until the *ibreek* is empty. It's filled once again and the process is repeated. The dancing and loud music continue into the early morning.

In addition to the beauty of the land and the hospitality of the culture, my country has a proud and ancient past. Lebanon traces its history back to Noah's son, Ham, and his Canaanite descendants. Caught between the empires of the Fertile Crescent on the north and of Egypt to the south, they were squeezed into a small strip of land on the Mediterranean coast and became the famed Phoenician navigators of the ancient world. The cities of Sidon and Tyre were their ports. Often history saw them dominated by one or another of the powerful empires surrounding them: Syria or Egypt; Assyria or Babylon; Persia, Greece or Rome. In the biblcal times of the kings of Israel and

Judah, these Canaanite descendants could be at different times either a blessing or a curse. Hiram, king of Tyre, was a beloved friend of David and provided him and his son, Solomon, with lumber from the beautiful cedars of Lebanon for the construction of the temple in Jerusalem. During later times of the divided kingdom, however, the pagan religious practices of these non-covenant Canaanite people were often a snare for God's people. The politically expedient marriage of King Ahab to the wicked Jezebel, daughter of the king of Tyre and Sidon, brought spiritual adultery and then divine wrath to God's people. In New Testament times, Jesus himself ministered to some of the faithful God-fearers along the Syro-Phoenician coasts. As Christianity expanded from the eastern Mediterranean world, Lebanon too felt the impact of the gospel. But with the rise of Islam in the seventh century, Christianity became a minority religion. The age of the Crusades saw a temporary reintroduction of Christian hegemony that gave way to the Muslim Ottoman Empire that continued into the twentieth century.

The modern country of Lebanon owes its origins to the spoils of World War I. Siding with the losing Axis powers, the once great Ottoman Empire of the eastern Mediterranean collapsed and finally came to an end. As the League of Nations made an attempt to further peace and justice in the emerging modern world, France was given a mandate that included the territory of Lebanon. Shortly thereafter, as World War II was slowly coming to a close in 1943, the Lebanese people seized the moment and claimed independence on November 22 of that year. The modern state of Lebanon was born. It was a unique Arab nation in that it had a slight majority Christian population represented by numerous branches of the faith, living in harmony and peace with the many varied sects of the Muslim faith, as well as, the Jews. The post World War II era saw many radical changes in the Middle East. Turkey was well along the pathway of becoming a secular state; the global impact and political ramifications of Middle East oil were becoming obvious; the state of Israel had declared independence in 1948; and in painful ways, the peoples and cultures of the area were becoming aware that they were still living in the Middle Ages while the rest of the world had moved into the twentieth century and modern times. The Lebanese government and people were more eager than most to move ahead into the promising world of industrialization and technology.

As Arab Christians with pro-western sympathies, my family and I shared with great anticipation all the promises of peace and prosperity the modern world was offering. For us, the United States was in many ways a role model and shining example after which we wished to pattern our own country and lives. As children we would see on our TV American cowboy shows, such as Bonanza, and would almost feel inspired by the tough moral standards that seemed to be the foundation of living the good life as it appeared on a western ranch in the happy and peaceful and prosperous country of the United States. There seemed to be a cultural contrast for us as we watched the "good guys" always winning out over the "bad guys." We imbibed the philosophy and worldview that life will be good and the rewards great when you fight for the right.

Lebanon was beautiful. As a child I grew up loving the land of old-world customs; the land of peaceful pastoral lifestyles; a land eager to move forward among the nations of the world into a promising new age. Would I be like my shepherd grandfather and enjoy the gentle life of a mountain village? Or would I seek my way in the cosmopolitan opportunities that I saw around me in Beirut? A child's mind and imagination will jump from one dream to another. And so it was with my own plans and ideas for the future. Whatever my ideas for that future might have been, the hopes and expectations were always high because I had dreams of the good life in Lebanon. I was a child and Lebanon was beautiful!

Chapter 2
First-Born, A Spoiled Son

*In Middle Eastern culture, it is both a privilege and a responsibility
to be the first-born son. And so it is that I entered the world with the
spoiling effects of privilege and the honorable work of responsibility.
My life would see success and failure on both counts.*

Elie 2 years old with parents and sister Georgette

It was a cool October night in the village of Ablah, located near the Bekaa valley of Lebanon. Everything was calm outside and the smell of the earth was refreshing after an early evening rain. Out of nowhere, gunshots disturbed the deep silence that extended into the mountains, its echoes traveling as far as the next village. Men who lived nearby left their houses and rushed outside to find out what was going on. On a nearby hill stood my father. The rifle he had just fired was resting on his shoulder. The loud sound of laughter bursting out of him had its origin in the bottom of his heart. "What's going on?" one of the men asked him, wondering if some act of violence had just taken place. "It's a boy! It's a boy! Elie is born!" my father answered boisterously. "I have a son. It's a boy." In the culture of Lebanon, parents are very proud to have a boy as their first-born. The first-born son has special privileges and responsibilities that are understood as his birthright. As a first-born son, I was regarded as a sign of the beginning of my father's strength and as the opener of my mother's womb. But I must honestly admit that the honor and privileges of my standing as first-born son tended to spoil me. There were times when I acted like a petty potentate at home. I would order my siblings around at will. My sisters would bring me the water jug and pour the water into my mouth if I ordered them to do it. They would remove my shoes from my feet at my command and even groom my hair and my fingernails. Despite my air of superiority, my sisters loved me and I deeply loved them.

Even my mother could not escape the pain of my rude and demanding behavior. After I was born, four sisters were added to our family. When my mother was expecting her sixth child, I found myself waiting and hoping for a brother.

I was seven years old when my mother gave birth to my fifth sister. I remember standing bedside and counting on my fingers the number of sisters I had. It was an entire handful! Tears came to my eyes and I blurted out to my mother, "You promised me that you would get me a brother. You lied to me!" I wasn't much encouragement to my mother at the time; she burst into tears and so did my father. Having five girls was a burden to a family. My parents thought they were unlucky and that it was some sort of a curse on our family.

Please understand, none of my spoiled behavior was ever intended to damage family solidarity or cause hurt to others. It was an expected role within the culture. In fact, the position of privilege as first-born son actually carried with it strong cultural responsibilities. Even as a child, I was often responsible for my siblings, whether at home, at school, or on the playground. It was understood in our society that my position of privilege carried a life-long burden to be the go-to person when any family member had a problem or a need. It would always be my responsibility to counsel and assist family members for the rest of my life. This meant that I would have to set high goals for myself. I would need to be able to support any needs that my grandparents, parents, or immediate family members might ever have, be they material, psychological, or physical. It was necessary for me to have ambitions, to harbor and accomplish dreams not merely for myself, but also for my extended family and for my country. These expectations for the first-born son would become very weighty and even dangerous for me as a young adult, but as a child I understood them in a more self-centered way. It was actually something of an inward arrogance coupled with a youthful inflation of self-importance.

The responsibilities as first-born were somewhat simple when I was young, but even these proved to be very stressful for me. The children in our family eventually numbered eight with the addition of two more boys. Because I was the oldest, it was assumed that I would be responsible for watching over all of my sisters and brothers. I remember once when Andre was three years old. My sisters were holding his hand as we crossed the road on the way to the store. He had let go of their hands and walked behind us as we crossed the road. Suddenly, I heard him crying loudly because he had been hit by a car. I was terrified as people around me rushed to help him. I felt so guilty and responsible for what had happened that I began to cry. I could see that my brother's leg had been broken when the car struck him. It was swollen and turning red and blue. When my parents arrived, they were distraught but all I thought about was whether they would blame or punish me. Even though this was a very serious incident, I still had confidence that no matter what I did, in the end, everyone would be kind and merciful to me simply because I was the oldest son.

Although I would not want to have lost any of my sisters or brothers, that did not stop me from selfishly wanting to be at the center of my parents' attention. I would even pretend that I was sick, knowing that they would pamper me. I often used this trick on them because it worked for me to get everything I needed or, should I say, wanted. Most of the time I did this just to hear them say, "We love you and care for you." In my culture and in my family, it was hard for anyone to express his or her love with words. People would do wonderful things for you, but they could not find it in themselves to use the words to say that they loved or cared for you. I regularly longed for this verbal assurance from my parents. I knew how much they loved me through their actions, but I wanted to hear it said out loud.

The favoritism shown toward the first-born son was especially manifested in those summer months when we visited my grandparents in our native village. In so many ways their affection and special regard for me encouraged my spoiled behavior. From the time of our arrival in the village, everyone seemed to give me more attention than they gave to the rest of my siblings. That pleased me. I knew that whatever I asked for would be given me by any one of them, beginning with my grandfather and grandmother, then my four uncles and two aunts. When I was younger, I often went with my grandmother or an aunt to meet my shepherd grandfather for lunch in the mountain pastures. His eyes would light up when he saw me. He would never eat until I had eaten first and even if there were others with me, I was the first one he fed. We had a very special relationship.

In the Lebanese culture, love is shown more by deed than by word. Discipline and corrective actions caused confusion within me, especially when it came from my parents. It was difficult for me to understand some of my father's harsh ways of dealing with me. My father was in the military service so he was often gone for many days and nights. When he was at home, his attitude and conduct often reflected the rough and tough ways of life in the military. His way of showing love was to be demanding and to push us hard to perform well in every aspect of life, especially at school.

Once I returned from school holding my report card in my hand. I was very proud and pleased with the effort I had put in to get the 4th rank in a class of 35 students. I entered the house and showed my dad the grades I had received and stated proudly, "I am 4th in my class!" His reaction was very shocking, a real surprise to me. He shouted, "You could have done better and had the first rank!" He sent me to the bedroom where I threw myself down on my bed and cried my eyes out. I shouted, "I hate school. I hate school. I don't want to go to school any more." I didn't know that my father was standing outside my door and heard what I said. He came into the room and used his belt to confirm the lesson, adding to my pain and misunderstanding. I was further required to kneel in the corner for one hour. I felt was scared and unsure if I was still loved. I wondered why he was doing this to me. As a child, I did not realize it was actually his love working itself out in the desire to help me excel and succeed in my life. The "tough love" disciplinary style of an army officer father was particularly hard for a child to grasp. The spoiled first-born son did not understand.

This incident turned me against school and made me hate studying. It also made me hate my sister Georgette who was one year younger than me, but who was very clever and got the highest grades. Everyone always compared me to her and emphasized how much better my sister was at school than me. So I responded like the spoiled child I was then. From that time on, my grades deteriorated. I made no effort to work hard on my schoolwork. When I got home from school in the afternoon, I would throw my book bag on the floor. This would upset my mother and she would shout at me and ask, "Elie, why are you doing this? Eat something and then start working on your lessons. I just want to see you open your book and learn." "I did all my work in school," I would respond curtly. Since my mother was illiterate, she could not help me with the work or verify the progress of my learning. She actually hired a relative to tutor my sister and me. The tutor realized that my sister was a better student than me, which really upset my parents. As the oldest boy, I was supposed to be the best. My mother was always shouting at me, but I responded by becoming more and more rebellious. I was determined to quit school early and find a job for myself, any job by which I could feel I was a man and accomplishing something beneficial.

Imagine how difficult my mother's situation was having to deal with eight children while my father was away most of the time with the army. She was forced to yell at us a lot—our house was always full of the noise. Sometimes, in desperation, my mother would lock us all in one room and put me in charge of all my brothers and sisters while she went to the store to buy groceries. She would tell us that she would be back in one hour. After she left, I would put a newspaper under the door and force the key from the outside lock to fall onto the newspaper. Then I would pull the key inside, open the door, let myself out, and then lock the door again on my siblings, leaving and taking the key with me. I would go play with my friends until it was time for my mother to return home. I would bribe my siblings with some candy so that they would not mention to my mother that I had left them alone. It was more important to me at those times to have fun playing rather than accepting my responsibility and helping my mother

Wanting to have fun sometimes led to childish pranks that went too far. I remember playing with my best friend, Akram, a Shia Muslim, and several other boys. We had taken some matches from home and were playing with them in the garden by our house. I saw a big gas truck that was parked at the side of the road. It was leaking gas and I saw an opportunity to create something bigger. I turned to my friend and said, "I need to go get some gas to make this fire bigger." He actually encourage me, "Let's do it." But when we got to the truck he got scared and said, "Hurry up, Elie, before anyone sees us." The bottle I had brought along to collect the gas had a small flame in it and when I tried to get some of the fuel, the gas truck caught on fire. There was a small puddle of water nearby and I tried flicking some water on the fire, but it was futile. I was so scared that I ran away and hid instead of seeking help. All of my friends ran for cover. Fortunately, there were some men nearby who saw the flames and were able to put out the fire before the truck exploded. My friends and I were never caught or punished. The seriousness of my actions didn't change my attitude as the spoiled child.

The cultural norms of privilege and responsibility that came with the status of first-born son created in me a combination of weaknesses and strengths. The privileges and honor that tended to favor me and thereby foster the conduct of a spoiled child. And yet the deference to my role helped to produce some positive emotional and social skills. I felt a strong sense of attachment to family and culture that came with the confidence of belonging. This made it easy for me to make friends and engage socially. However, the responsibilities as eldest son would regularly overwhelm me with demands I felt inadequate to meet. From the earliest days of my youth, I could sense the onus of accountability that my privileged position carried with it. At the same time these seemingly demanding requirements also developed within me a passion and ambition in life, influencing others around me to share those goals. These were the beginnings of leadership traits. There were both highs and lows, gains and losses, victories and defeats when I was a child and during my early adult years. This combination of failures and successes would be a pattern not only as a child seeking to cope with the first-born role, but also in the years ahead as I faced the challenges of civil war in Lebanon.

Beyond the love of my country and the cultural duties of eldest child, I was negatively impacted by the failure of my religious upbringing to grasp the personal and powerful elements of the Christian faith. This is a very important part of my story.

Chapter 3
Cultural Christianity

God, we are told, has no grandchildren. The value of Christianity is in direct proportion to the measure of one's first-hand and lively experience of it. But our family practice of the faith was little more than dead, formal tradition. Our under-standing and knowledge of God was limited to input from the priest and the culture.

Elie with Parents and Siblings

In Lebanon, as with some other countries of the world, one's religious association is clearly indicated on their national identity card. Unlike western countries where religious identification is a personal and moral choice, the identification listed on the national identity card has more to do with tradition or culture or social standing than with individual spiritual convictions. I was identified as a Christian in the Roman Catholic Church. Such membership for me was indeed cultural, even political, rather than a matter of embracing ultimate, life-changing truth. I grew up with a significant pride in my Christian heritage, but I had no real understanding of or commitment to the meaning of being a follower of Christ. My faith provided me with community identification and a sense of social belonging, but it did not provide me with a worldview that actually incorporated God into the historical realities around me, the moral issues within me, or eternal judgments toward me. Both in understanding and in practice, my cultural Christian faith was rather cold. I understood the difference between right and wrong, well in part, anyway. I had a natural knowledge of God. I knew that He existed, but not much more than that! This cultural approach to the faith gave me not only a sense of identity and belonging, but it also gave me a certain type of security or hope both in this world and for the world beyond death.

Lebanon has many different religions and denominations. Even among the Christians there are numerous groups from various historical backgrounds and theological viewpoints— Arameans, Chaldeans, Latins, Maronites, Melkites, Syrian Rite, Armenian Orthodox, Greek Orthodox, Syrian Orthodox, and Protestants. My family tradition was in the

Roman Catholic Church, although the practice of our faith was not regular. During the summer months in Deir Mimas we attended services more often as part of the social fabric of a small community, but during the school year in Beirut, we were not faithful in regularly attending mass. Our practice of the faith was mostly limited to special holy days or religious events such as marriages, baptisms, confirmations, and funerals. Even these events were more social happenings than truly meaningful spiritual experiences in our lives.

True religion is a matter of the heart. As a child, I did not properly understand that the formalism of tradition was only meant to provide a picture of and point toward the spiritual realities behind the outward forms. I gained little from attending church. On those Sundays when my mother would dress us up and take us to St Michael's Catholic Church, the largest and most famous Catholic Church in Beirut, I understood almost nothing of the service. I marveled at the architecture, the stained-glass windows, and the richly colored robes of the priests. Without realizing it, I was only being trained to be a faithful follower of a traditional and national religion rather than being taught to know the living, personal God of transforming relationships.

Despite my intellectual failure to approach God through the forms and traditions of my church, God was beginning to stir in my heart and to prick my conscience. As I entered adolescence, not only did I sense a change in my body, but in my way of thinking as well. My own physical changes had to be faced along with the changes and conflicts arising at the same time in Lebanon. Many things were happening in the world that I couldn't fully grasp. All around me were the political maneuvering of various religions and nationalities.

Difficult questions began to trouble my mind: Where did I come from? Why am I alive? What is valuable in life? Where are we all going? What happens after death? Although I had little direction, I found I was sensitive to spiritual things. I woke up one night and I looked outside the window at the soccer playground and I saw a very strange thing. There in the middle of the playground was a very long illuminated pillar. It was so tall that I could not believe my eyes. For a moment I thought that I was dreaming. I rubbed my eyes and looked in the mirror, then looked out the window once more. It was still there. The top was reaching all the way to the sky and there was light in the sky. I was so frightened that I ran to my room and covered myself with the blanket. I had such difficulty going back to sleep. I kept thinking of what I saw. Early in the morning, I went back and looked out the window, wondering if the pillar would still be there. I saw nothing. I told my mother about it, but with a big smile on her face she assured me that it was a dream and that I had had too much for supper. I knew what I had seen was real, though, and it just caused more questions. The most serious questions were about God: Does God really exist? If so, where is he? What does he do?

When the time came for me to have my first communion, I attended the required teaching beforehand. The Catholic school I attended prepared students to have their first communion during the same month every year. My mom was so excited the time had come for me to make my first communion and said to me, "Catholics should have a first communion ceremony so that they can become Christians and can go to heaven." Both at home and at school I received instructions about the doctrines of the mass and although I did not really understand, I was willing to obey my parents' wishes and to fulfill all the requirements.

I put on the white robe my mom had purchased for the occasion and we headed off to St. Michael's Church where the ceremony would take place. I found myself standing in a queue of about thirty other children, all of them in white robes, each waiting for his or her turn to receive their first communion. I got to the front and stood before the priest. I opened my mouth as he was about to put a round thing into it. I was expecting a sweet taste, but to my surprise it was quite bitter. I swallowed it with considerable difficulty. Because God had been stirring deep in my heart with "bigger" questions about life and faith and the world, I was disappointed that some special experience or revelation did not materialize. There had to be something more. I could not help but observe that my parents and many of our relatives sitting in the church all had big smiles on their faces, very happy and pleased that I had been forgiven. A big celebration awaited me when we returned home. I remember receiving lots of gifts, but my questions had not been answered. The experience of this most sacred of Christian practices did not bring me closer to knowing God.

Households and villages all had their patron saints. The traditions of the Catholic Church at least tolerated and often encouraged both prayers and festivals for their honor. Every year in the middle of September we waited expectantly for the feast held for Saint Mama, the guardian and patron saint of our native village, Deir Mimas, as well as, the Litani River. This event was more of a social and cultural celebration rather than a religious holiday. The celebration was held in a monastery of the Orthodox Church in Lebanon. Saint Mama was martyred in 275 AD and is remembered as Holy Mama. He was a shepherd from Cyprus who preached to the animals of the wilderness. Tradition says that one friendly lion followed him and licked his limbs. When the Aurelian persecutors came to stone Holy Mama, he sent the lion back to his lair sobbing. Saint Mama is often pictured with a lion and is considered the saint of guardians, orphans, and torture victims.

At the entrance of every home was a statue of a different saint. At times people would gather around the statue and pray. I always wondered why people were praying to this statue while people in other buildings chose to pray to others. I started asking about this, but it only opened a wider door of confusion for me. When I asked why the different saints, I was told that each family had a different saint as their patron and that they had to pray to him or her to receive the blessings of salvation and redemption. These saints were also intercessors before God on our behalf and were counted on to mediate for us in order to avoid the receiving of curses. Many nights during the evening gatherings, the subject of saints aroused conflicts and disputes between relatives. Each sided for their patron and bragged about him or her. When I asked for information about these saints, I was dumbfounded to find out that even their followers had very little knowledge about them.

Even though I continued to be confused by all the arguments, I followed what was the cultural norm: I finally sided with one saint over the others and considered him to be my patron saint. The prophet Elijah is my namesake. He is the bold Old Testament prophet who confounded the prophets of Baal at Mount Carmel. He is the mystical lover of Yahweh who heard the voice of God in the gentle breeze. He is the one who was taken to heaven alive in a chariot of fire; and he appeared with Jesus on the Mount of Transfiguration in New Testament times. Many parents in the Middle East and in Eastern Europe name their sons after him—Ilya is the common Slavonic name and Elie the French form. The Hebrew name is Eliyahu and means "My God is Yahweh." As my patron saint, I would be reminded of his passion for the Lord, the answered prayers of a righteous man, and God's faithful provision to a faithful prophet. It gave me a sense of security; I felt that I was pleasing God and being a good Christian. Still, the traditions of cultural Christianity never satisfied the cold void in my mind and heart. Unanswered questions remained and that aching hunger was not satisfied.

In addition to finding it difficult to grasp the spiritual realities of God through the fog of Christian formalism and traditionalism, Middle Eastern culture corrupts Christianity with a powerful influence of superstitions and the occult. Like everyone around us, our family practiced these cultural customs that at their best are meaningless and at their worst are downright demonic. Once, when I was very ill with strep throat and had a very high fever, the doctor prescribed antibiotics in the form of injections. My parents took me daily to a special nurse who was assigned to give me the injection. This procedure was so scary to me that I would resist with all my might. My father decided that it was all too much. He couldn't stand to see me suffer like that every day so he took me to a sheik to figure out if someone had cast an "evil eye" on me, causing me to suffer so. This is a common belief among Muslims and they convinced my parents to pursue this possible cause of my sickness. Protection from the "evil eye" is sought after diligently. On the back of trucks or on the door of a house one can see the picture of an eye with an arrow drawn through it. This talisman is believed to protect whatever property on which it's placed from harm by anyone who is envious. Small children often carry protection against the "evil eye" with them in the form of small blue pearls. Women wear gems to divert the "evil eye" so that its glance can do no harm. The Middle East is full of such superstitious ideas and cultic practices.

When I was taken to the sheik, he heated a special kind of metal in a melting point, said some verses from the Koran along with special prayers, and finally poured the molten metal into an empty frying pan over my head. The sheik interpreted the shape of the hardening solder. In my case, the metal reflected the shape of a woman. My parents studied the form, trying to recognize or remember who she was, believing she might have been the cause of my illness.

Fortune telling was a part of daily life in the Middle East as another expression of superstition in the culture. My superstitious Aunt, always fearful and curious about her future, took me along with her children to a fortuneteller. I recall the thick incense, the speaking in other tongues, and the pictures of saints. I was afraid. And the woman only looked frightened herself and puzzled, as she attempted to peer into the future with the help of dark spirits. I knew even then with only my cultural Christianity that this was somehow wrong.

As I grew older and the political and social situations in Lebanon grew worse, I longed for answers to life's biggest questions and for encouragement in my life. I found no answers or solutions in my practice of cultural Christianity so I followed the advice of some friends and went with them to a fortuneteller. I remembered my earlier experience with my aunt. I felt my heart beating very fast and a great deal of fear mixed with excitement as I entered the room of this fortune-teller. She asked me, "Son, what do you need to know?" She was an old woman and the room was filled with the pictures of saints and the thick smoke of incense, exactly as I remembered from before. I answered her question, telling her I needed to know more about my future and myself. I wanted to know who were my friends and who were my enemies. She asked for a payment of about fifty Lebanese pounds and then she began to talk to someone who was not visible to me. She was able to tell me the make and color of my car, but nothing more. She said the spirits didn't show her anything further. I was very angry and went away without ever coming back. I felt that I had been cheated. I would like to tell you I had learned a lesson and this would be my last experience with a fortuneteller, but the pressures of war and the spiritual void in my understanding would drive me once again to seek counsel from the dark side.

During my childhood, followers of different religions were mutually friendly. They respected each other's beliefs and practices and lived together in harmony most of the time. I recall one specific incident when we were living in the military apartments in Beirut that illustrates the good will that existed between so many people of different faiths. The family living next to us was Muslim. Everyone called the woman Hajji, a common term applied to a woman who has made the pilgrimage to Mecca as required at least once in a lifetime for those who practice Islam seriously. Because we lived so close together and our balconies faced each other, I became familiar with her practices of daily prayer. One day, being a four-year-old boy who liked to copy what he saw adults doing, I pulled out a small rug, put it on the balcony, and knelt down and started praying as I had seen her do. After a while I would stand up and then kneel down again. It happened one morning that Hajji saw me from her balcony and started shouting, "Em Elie, em Elie." My mother rushed to the balcony fearing that something bad had happened. When she saw what I was doing, she started laughing so loudly that everyone in the house followed the sound of her laughter to see what was going on. Hajji was pleased to see me imitating her. She called out to my mom, "I wish that Elie were my son." This is the way we lived—a tolerant respect and a friendly harmony between those of different religions.

Our training from the church did not help us understand that while respect and harmony between Christians and other faiths may well be proper conduct, it had not taught us that all religions are not created equal. There were times when respect bordered on syncretism. We did not understand that cultural harmony based on a denial of the real differences in revealed truth between religions is a fragile state of existence. Nor did the church teach us about the deceptions and spiritual dangers of the occult world and other religions.

With all the effort I made to understand and know more about God, I had a very limited knowledge. I found no one around me who could explain things or answer my questions. God was unknown to me, to my parents, and to all the people around me. I believed that he was very distant from people, that he was old, and that he punished people who sin and do not obey. Once I was even told that he would choke children if they lied! Cultural Christianity was good enough at that time. We were confident that the priest had the powers to forgive our sins. We were proud of being part of the biggest religion in the world; the Pope was our hero; and we were better than the others. But cultural Christianity would not be good enough to keep us in touch with God during the rapidly approaching catastrophes for Lebanon and the Middle East.

There are serious problems when one's Christian faith and training are merely traditional, mainly social, and markedly cultural rather than matters of personal conviction and spiritual reality. While faith should have given me a relationship with God that would help me hold a worldview according to His perspective of the soon-to-happen chaos in the Middle East, a chaos that would spill over into Lebanon; my social Christianity would actually add to the partisan attitudes of anger and hatred that began to grow in my heart. While my faith should have introduced me to a knowledge of God that would emphasize his mercy and forgiveness, as well as his power for overcoming sin and living a holy life, my perception of God only left me with guilt over my own human weaknesses and the ethnic, religious hatreds I was incapable of conquering. Cultural religions do not provide real comfort or satisfactory answers to the world's tragedies. Cultural Christianity failed to meet my needs by failing to connect me with God in a living relationship. My religion was little more than a political and cultural statement on my national identification card.

These are my roots: the beautiful land of Lebanon where my life as the first-born son in an Arab Christian family began in the middle of the twentieth century. How could I ever have imagined what the future really held in store for me? No one could have told me that God himself was watching, not only the whole of the Middle East, but even me individually and personally. It never entered my thinking that his ways are not our ways and his thoughts are not our thoughts. While there were many storm clouds gathering on the horizon of the Middle East, it never would have occurred to me to ask what their impact on my world and my life might be.

PART II
CONFLICTS AND CRISES ARISE

Chapter 4
Conflicts Raise Questions

The worldview of my childhood would be thrown into turmoil by the events unfolding in the Middle East. Profound questions of "Why?" would overwhelm the happy innocence of my youth.

In the last half of the twentieth century, Lebanon became the innocent bystander, victimized by the religious and political upheavals in the Middle East. Our country became the hostage of more powerful governments; an escape and retreat for innocent refugees; the staging ground for new radical movements and terrorism; and the frequent battleground in Israel's fight for her own purpose and survival. With roots in Christian charity, my homeland sought to help the Palestinian refugees who rewarded that kindness by eventually hastening the formation of a house divided. The ensuing civil war was officially ended in 1990, but the wounds have never been fully healed. From an historical perspective, it seems there was no escaping the inevitable conflicts that would arise as Zionism gave birth to Israel and the Muslim Middle East, as if rudely awakened from the dull sleep of the Middle Ages, gave birth to a reinvigorated radical Islamic response to the modern world. Poor little Lebanon on the northern border of Israel was caught in the crossfire.

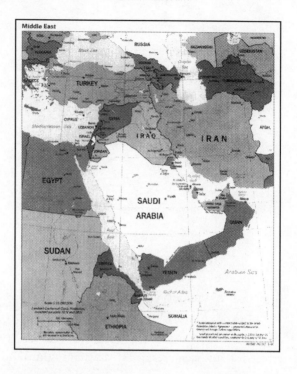

Early seeds for the demise of Christian-majority Lebanon were planted and began to grow with Israel's war of independence in 1948. At that time Palestinian refugees numbering in the many tens of thousands streamed across the border into Lebanon. Lebanon demonstrated Arabic solidarity and Christian compassion by receiving them. This influx of angry and religiously motivated refugees began to have a profound impact on the social and political landscape of my homeland. A fresh and powerful leaven of radical religious hatreds and ethnic divisions was being introduced into the already fragile social, political, and religious environment of our young country. By the time I was born in 1962, the Middle East was already a seething cauldron, brewing with incipient radicalism and terrorism as the religious and ethnic differences spilled over into political agendas, manipulated by the geopolitical cold war and the clash between lands still living in the mindset of the Middle Ages and those well along the pathway of the modern world. In 1967, these tensions exploded in the amazing Six-day War when a confederacy of surrounding Arab nations launched a surprise and unprovoked attack on Israel. Israel's spectacular and swift victory left her with great spoils of land and prestige, but the humiliation and losses of the Muslim Arab populations only served to more finely crystallize and more severely amplify tensions and hatreds. Lebanon became increasingly the haven for fleeing Palestinians and a proliferating number of radical groups.

This situation became much worse when, in September of 1970, Jordan's King Hussein began the work of expelling all Palestinian refugees from his country. He did this as a defensive response of self-preservation against the armed PLO (Palestine Liberation Organization) factions that had jeopardized the stability of his own country and government in the civil unrest of militarized radicals known as the Black September War. Again, Lebanon became the last place of refuge for these radical elements, now numbering in the thousands. The confederate Arab nations were themselves rejecting these Palestinians and mercilessly allowed Lebanon to become their dumping ground. The political and social impact of these violent refugees in Beirut and southern Lebanon was devastating to the stability and tranquility of the Lebanese people. Internal tensions mounted and there was vicious fighting between the Lebanese army and the Palestinians. Any discerning observer could see that Lebanon was breaking apart and that its leadership, a combination of corrupt and incompetent people, was doing little to deal with this critical internal division. The government was losing control of its own territory and destiny.

The influx of large numbers of violent PLO elements aggravated what was already a fragile working relationship between Christians and Muslims in both the government and society as a whole. There had been civil unrest between some groups in the 1950's. The slight majority Christian population at that time rapidly became a minority. The radical elements of the growing refugee Muslim population created heightened tensions and armed battles between these two religiously based political parties. As the Palestinian guerillas began to effectively implement their own foreign policy goals, particularly violence against the state of Israel, there were deep repercussions for the increasingly tenuous Lebanese government. Yasser Arafat used his new strongholds in the south of the country to stage terrorist raids into Israel. These border attacks naturally drew retaliatory responses from Israel, but the dueling between the PLO and Israel was not a resolution of the matters between the warring parties. The result was tremendous suffering for the Christians of southern Lebanon. Caught in the crossfire, many were killed and their homes and property suffered great destruction.

The cordial relationship between the Christian and Muslim sectors within Lebanon suddenly exploded into violent conflict. To grasp how this could happen so rapidly, you must understand a subtle aspect of Muslim character and culture. Middle Eastern ideas of honor and pride are blended with a display of courtesy in such a way that outward demonstrations of kindness may often conceal very different attitudes and feelings hidden deep within. These two contrasting traits are called *zahiri*, what is displayed and seen on the outside of the person, and *batani,* that which is held in secret at the deeper levels within that motivate an individual. As a result, the explosive situations developing in our country were complicated by the psyche of Middle Eastern culture and character along with the political situation.

From my personal perspective and that of my family living in Beirut during those years, the unfolding events were truly catastrophic. Being the son of a Lebanese military officer only intensified my confusion and fear. For the first time in my life I felt afraid to be part of the family of a soldier. Rather than being respected for working to stabilize the situation, we actually became special objects of hatred to the warring religious and political factions. My mother took extra precautions every time we went outside the house. We always walked close to walls and even slept at my uncle's house for many nights out of fear that our building would be a target for attack. I remember the first time God saved me from such an attack. I had just stepped out onto the balcony of our apartment in Beirut. The moment I set foot onto the balcony, a bullet from the rifle of a Palestinian sniper struck the wall just above my head. My mother screamed, "Elie, get down." As I quickly dropped to the floor, she rushed out and dragged me inside the house, locked all the doors and windows, and made us all sit in the one part of the apartment she considered to be safe. She warned us all never to go out on the balcony again.

Only when you have experienced this kind of situation personally is it possible to fully appreciate the impact such social chaos has on your everyday life. As more and more violence and killings were taking place, I watched relatives, neighbors, and family friends making plans to protect their families in case of danger—where to run, where to hide, the importance of having clothes ready, and cans of food stored. Their conversations shifted one hundred and eighty degrees from what I used to hear. After being accustomed to sounds of their loud laughter and happy songs, I now saw only somber faces and heard only concern about the killings and violence that were becoming a part of daily life. Everywhere, fear and uncertainty continually replaced contentment. Anger and hatred soon followed. Being so young I was not able to understand the whole situation. I tried to get answers for my many questions: Why is there a war? Why is my Dad away? Why are we fighting against the Palestinians since they stood with us against Israel? I received no satisfactory answers and I could only struggle inwardly with my own confusion and fear.

When on October 6, 1973, Egypt and Syria launched the coordinated surprise attack against Israel that became the Yom Kippur War, the days of a truly independent and free Lebanon were in extreme jeopardy and coming to a sad end. By the time the war ended, Lebanon was little more than a puppet to Syria and the nations of the Arab world, a slave and a pawn to the radical PLO elements (one of the terror arms of the Palestinian refugees), and the ongoing battlefield between Israel and her many enemies. The nation was truly a house divided. Citizen allegiances were scattered and mixed between many religious, ethnic, and political parties. The international community of nations little understood and gave only lip service concern for the carnage and destruction that mounted in my once beautiful homeland.

While these conflicts and wars made life increasingly wretched, my questions born out of confusion and fear continued to rise within me, but they remain unanswered. I struggled with the idea that Israel alone was not to blame for our misery and the troublesome internal radicals bore significant blame for the trials we endured. I well remember an incident during that 1973 war when we were watching fighter jets over the city and the mountains to our east. We were able to clearly see Israeli and Syrian planes as they soared overhead and shot at one another, each trying to score against the other and at the same time avoid being hit. We played a game as we watched these air battles, trying to predict which plane would win and which one would be hit and fall. When a Syrian jet was destroyed and crashed to the ground, however, our anti-Israeli sympathies were revealed as the atmosphere became filled by disappointment and tense with fear. People were glued to their radios for all of the latest developments. Many were saying that Israel was the enemy and could not be trusted. When I would ask my questions concerning why the Jews were our enemy, the answer was only that they wanted to take Arab land. Even then I thought the answer seemed inadequate for my question and I continued to doubt what I was being told.

Because my father had been relocated to the southern part of Lebanon, he had an opportunity to build a house for our family in our hometown of Deir Mimas. He moved us back to our native village in 1974. Little did we realize that this move would be like jumping from the frying pan of the mounting chaos in Beirut into the fires of social, religious, and military tensions on the border with Israel. I would soon be entering my teen years and could no longer be shielded from many of the realities that were happening around me. It would have been difficult for anyone to shelter me from the impact of events in this now international hot spot, even if they had wanted to do so. The response of fear yielding to anger; anger growing into hatred; and hatred plotting revenge and retaliation would find a place in my heart along with my questions. I was ripe for the pickings by groups that were choosing sides as the divisions of countryside partisanships increased. The mounting tensions between Muslims and Christians; the danger of retaliatory raids by Israel against the PLO were just two of the threats now lurking in our very neighborhood. The failure of the Lebanese government to deal with divisions in the country caused by the radical leftist elements now disrupted the life of my beautiful Lebanon. I struggled to make sense of the conflicts around me with no hope.

By 1975 the divided agendas and allegiances of the various parties now residing in Lebanon had so disrupted the political, military, religious, ethnic, and social fabric of Lebanon that total civil war broke out. It is difficult to relate or even understand the events and their cause and effect relationships that brought about the collapse of a state government and a national way of life. The actions and reactions of those internal groups with conflicting intentions worked to create a chaos in which the society lost its cohesion and the God-ordained governmental responsibilities of order for the common good were abandoned.\ In Beirut, the ferment boiled over into killings on the streets and competing militias fought pitched battles in the city. Murders abounded and civil services were collapsing. Daily life in Beirut was truly dangerous. Radical military Palestinians set up checkpoints and killed many Christians when they were stopped.

The toll in human life and property destruction was staggering. The statistics for the Lebanese civil war estimate nearly a quarter of a million civilian fatalities with another million wounded, and countless millions displaced. Keep in mind that Lebanon is a small country and that most of these losses were suffered by the Christian segment of the population. It is difficult to convey the extent of our pain and losses as pent up hatreds erupted in religious persecutions and retaliations. Many thousands of innocent victims endured horrific and unexpected violence.

International efforts to resolve the out-of-control situation proved to have little effect and resulted in the government losing further control of its own people. A 1976 Arab summit arranged a ceasefire to be maintained by Syria and in 1978, the UN Security Council resolution established UNIFIL (United Nations Interim Force in Lebanon) which was to oversee the withdrawal of Israeli forces from the south of the country and the re-establishment of the Lebanese governmental authority. By now the government itself had come under the controlled of radical partisan elements. Government authority was divided and different sections of Beirut and Lebanon were controlled by warring factions. The PLO under Yasser Arafat used the southern areas of Lebanon as a base of attacks against Israel. Israel countered with frequent incursions into the country, raiding even as far north as Beirut. Peacekeeping efforts by such countries as France, Italy, and the United States ended in failure and sometimes tragedy. The terrible conditions of civil war continued from 1975 until 1990. The theoretical end to the Lebanese civil war was more a technicality of accepting the dangerous divisions of the status quo than the reality of national restoration and peace. To this day the political, religious, and ethnic rivalry dominating the Middle East continues to ravage and divide the social and political fabric of the country; and Israel is forced to cope daily with the reality of terrorist organizations, funded and encouraged by Arab states, using Lebanon as a safe haven and military launch point.

The concept of loyalty is very strong in the thinking of an Arab, but it is not necessarily linked to the modern Western concept of the nation state. The Middle Eastern Arab has passionate feelings of loyalty to family and clan; he will show intense allegiance to his Muslim religion and its leaders; and he can be strongly committed to political parties, factions, and philosophies. All of these passions often lead to a loyalty that is much greater than patriotism to a particular nation state or government. This cultural mindset has made it difficult to maintain a political unity among the Lebanese people. The division of loyalties, often in conflict with one another, has left patriotic, national allegiance far down the list of priorities, leading to the break-up a truly independent national existence in Lebanon.

This is a commentary, an interpretation of the historical events of my homeland as I experienced them. These are the facts of my young life. I struggled alone to make sense out of what was happening. I was frightened by the astounding events that ravaged the world around me. We literally dodged bullets on the streets of Beirut and daily worked just to survive. While the leaders of the world frantically labored with the complexity of the issues and circumstances, the heart and mind of this almost teenage boy were overwhelmed with confusion and unanswered questions. From childhood I had grown up thinking that the Jews in Israel were a great enemy. There had almost been the aura of a *boogey man* associated with our neighbors to the south and I would have been afraid to meet one of them on a dark street, but now it was the Palestinians who seemed most responsible for the terror and chaos all around me. What you do not understand, you fear. I began to feel toward the Palestinians as I used to feel toward the Jews. I could not understand why the Palestinians, whom we in Lebanon had befriended, were now the enemy tearing apart our beautiful land. They had made themselves enemies. Rather than gratefully accepting the help our country had offered them, they made themselves an internal hornets nest, spreading hate and misery—and division.

As I watched the fighting all around me, my personal ambitions for the future began to be transformed and I viewed things very differently. The strife of religious and political struggles in the Middle East had spilled over, resulting in the civil war for Lebanon. That battle jumped with ease into my own heart. There seemed to be no answers to my questions and no solutions to the problem of war . A profound sense of hopelessness settled on me and led to my desire to lash out; to fight back. Confusion and fear led to frustration and anger. My heart was set to actively defend what I thought was rightfully mine. Without really thinking about it, I was being drawn into the conflict that I actually hated. The months and years ahead would prove that I, a first-born son in Christian Lebanon, was not psychologically or spiritually prepared for the challenges I would be forced to face. I had moved beyond the internal confusion and fear caused by a civil war in my native Lebanon and made the journey to anger and hate. I took sides and became personally involved in the war.

Chapter 5
Death Behind My Door

My world was falling apart. And my heart was now being infected with anger and bitterness. I tried to solve the problems in my own strength and failed. I only found death behind my door.

Elie with Friends

When we moved in 1974 to our native village of Deir Mimas, it seemed at first to be a quiet haven from life in Beirut. I was busy with school and all of the activities of turning into a young man. Friends were to be had all around and the activities we shared were a constant stream of fun. I soon realized I wasn't in a haven. The religious and political divisions that had been tearing apart the Middle East, and now my beloved Lebanon, had seeped into the lives of everyone. The warlike partisanship now infiltrated our lives and our little village. Everyone took sides. I could see the effects of these divisions among my friends in how they would treat each other. Agenda-driven groups of young men formed based on their religious, political, and ethnic rivalries. The power of money played an important role since groups would pay young men to join them. The more they paid, the more members they were able to attract.

The groups of young men mimicked the partisan groups among the adults. As a soldier in the army, my father had to associate himself with one of these groups. He felt the need to patriotically defend his land, his village, his family, and his possessions. The people in the village divided into two factions, which completely changed the atmosphere of my village. Families who had always been friends, who had lived in peace for decades, suddenly became enemies. Tensions between families and neighbors escalated as their focus turned to the ideological differences, while respect for one another was tossed aside. The greater concern was over whom was going to succeed in forcing their views upon another. People felt threatened by those who were different. Each group wanted to control or destroy the values, belongings, and even the lives of others. Pride, bitterness, anger, fear, and finally hatred took hold of the hearts of the residents of Deir Mimas, as in all of Lebanon. Deep divisions and passionate partisan loyalties formed that eventually overwhelmed and took the lives of many.

My friends and I tried as best we could to live as normal as possible within these conditions, playing as we could, but well aware of the changes going on. We used to play together, but separate groups were beginning to form, just like within the country. I remember being out with one of my friends and someone rushing up to him to tell him to leave, quickly. They disappeared in a second. I went with other friends to swim in the river near our home and while we were there, we heard shots; then people screaming and running away. We were more curious to know where the shots were coming from then frightened so we got out of the water and snuck along the side of the river until we saw a group of young men training to shoot guns. To our surprise, two of our friends were in the group.

The next day, I asked these friends what they were doing training with guns; I wanted to know what was behind all this. One of them said, "We will free Palestine!" Another, "We will prevent Israel from taking more land." A third one said, "We want to defend our country!" And still someone else said, "We will be paid money." I was scared, but I wanted to do what they were doing. I wanted to carry a weapon and get paid for it. I knew for sure my parents would never allow me to join them. I had no idea for whom they were fighting; who was right or who was wrong, but I was ready to join them just to keep their friendship. I valued friendship more than I cared what my parents thought so when asked, I joined them and started to carry a weapon.

The civil war that began in Beirut in 1975 quickly spread to the south of the country where the depth of the civil rift became obvious as the Lebanese military itself began to break apart. Portions of the army were made up of mainly

Christian soldiers. These began to form sympathetic working relations with the IDF (Israeli Defense Forces) in an effort to stop the radical Muslim elements of the leftist factions such as the PLO. While the official government in Beirut was increasingly succumbing to the power and demands of the Palestinians and their sympathizers, a portion of the Lebanese military in the south of the country broke away and formed the FLA (Free Lebanon Army), siding with Israel and its attempts to deal with Palestinian violence. Its founder, Major Sa'ad Haddad, was officially dismissed and branded a traitor. The FLA was the precursor to the SLA (South Lebanese Army) of which I would eventually become an active and leading member.

In Beirut, Christians were being randomly singled out and killed by lawless Muslim mobs and Palestinian snipers. As the civil war spread from the city to the countryside and its villages, radical Islamic militias began to slaughter whole Christian villages. Among the many records of such viciousness, one of the early and most memorable is the Muslim attack on the village of Damour. Lying near the seacoast along the highway from Beirut to Sidon, this town became the target in January of 1976 of the PLO and its work of ethnic and religious cleansing. Christians and those suspected of inadequate sympathies for the Palestinian fight against Israel were targeted for death. An internet search for Damour will yield many articles dealing with the atrocities committed there. It is estimated that more than 500 were killed. When the International Red Cross went to bury the dead, it was necessary to count heads because so many of the bodies had been dismembered. On July 15, 1979 in Cannes, France, Zuhayer Muhsin, the military architect of this tragedy, was assassinated, but this gave little comfort to the survivors of this grizzly episode.

With such events taking place around us, it is understandable that those of us who were in villages of a Christian majority felt unsafe. Such religious and ethnic violence was festering at home in Deir Mimas and came fully into our reality one day when armed Palestinian Muslims were seen approaching our village. The army of Christian soldiers and men from the village formed a line of defense while the women and children ran to find shelter. My father and my uncles were Christian Lebanese soldiers. These Christian leaders had no option but to fight or die. The lessons of Damour and many other such incidents were our teachers and we knew this was a true crisis situation.

I remember the day so well. I was playing with my friends and sisters near the garden when I heard my mother with fear and urgency calling us to come home quickly. We could hear the unusual strain in her voice and ran to her at once. She had already gathered the most meager of provisions in preparation for our flight as refugees. "Elie," she said, "Carry the bread and hold your little sister's hand and watch over your other sisters. I will carry your two brothers." I tried to ask her what was going on, but there was no time for explanations or delay. She firmly commanded, "Just obey me. They are coming to kill us. Your father says we have to follow the other families and go to the next Christian village." She lifted my two brothers off the ground into her strong arms. As she started to run she called out to us, "Follow me, all of you, right now!"

I held the bread and my little sister's hand and as a young, good runner started running as fast as I could. My aunts and other relatives with children were following close behind us. My mother was heading toward the other end of the village. We were so scared and running as if we wanted to win some kind of race; it was literally a race for our lives. As we ran, our shoes would sometimes fall off and I dropped some of the bread too, but my mother said, "Do not stop no matter what. Just make sure all of your sisters are with you." Fear gave us more energy to run fast. We ran about ten miles. There was a one-mile long line of people fleeing, mainly women and children. The children were terrified and crying and many were shouting, "Hurry, hurry! We don't want to be killed!" Finally, we reached the neighboring Christian village. It made us feel a little more secure once we entered a house there. We stayed with three other families in that house, crowding my family into one of the little rooms. We had some of the bread we had brought with us, but not knowing how long we were going to be there my mother determined to ration our supply. "Each day we will eat a little portion of the bread. It will last longer that way."

This was one of those occasions when my being the first son was not a privilege, but rather a responsibility. I felt so inadequate to assure the safety and well being of all of my siblings. I wished with all my heart that my father were with us. We were not able to bring any extra clothes along. We were experiencing all the miserable conditions of being refugees. We lived like this for several weeks, all sitting together in that little room like sheep trapped in a barn. Life as a refugee was bathed in an aura of hopelessness and humility. As refugees, we were as in a pit, unable to help ourselves out, desperately in need, and very frightened. Anger rose among us as despair and a desire for justice…no, really vengeance…worked deeply into our psyche. Finally, aide arrived from Israel for all the nearby Christian villages. The Christians had sought help from the Israeli government and the Israeli Defense Force (IDF). We were supplied with food, shelter, and medicine. Israel also agreed to provide hundreds of Christians with weapons and training to fight so we could defend ourselves. A few months later, we returned to our village when my father sent for us. At last it was safe for us to return to our homes. The brave men had done a good job of defense.

The flight from Deir Mimas and so many other experiences in those early years of the civil war reached out and embroiled me personally in the many tragedies of that war. As a Lebanese Christian, it was altogether natural that I should resent the murder of Christians by radical Muslim Palestinian refugees in my country. And as the responsible oldest son entering his teen years, it was reasonable that I would want to prove my manhood by being willing to risk my own life for the protection of my family and our way of life. As I had experienced the dangers of warfare in Beirut, now I came to realize that the same ethnic and religious struggles were all around me, even in my village of Deir Mimas. There in the village I was finding my place in the local paramilitary groups that were forming. My commitment to and involvement in them increased as the dangers increased and increase they did.

I had made the journey from confusion to fear and from fear to hopelessness. The step to anger and then hate was quick and inevitable. These strong emotions, in response to the collapse of my world and my dreams, would now require action. So it was that I chose sides and then picked up arms to follow through on that decision. Upon returning home after this time of forced refugee status, life would never return to the carefree memories of my childhood. Now everyone was taking sides in the conflict. I was becoming defensive and reckless in my choices. Although I was still attending school, by 1978 I had determined to join the Free Lebanon Army (FLA) both as a defense and an offense for combating the Palestine Liberation Organization (PLO). Members of the FLA were mainly Christians who resented the armed radical Palestinian factions controlling southern Lebanon and West Beirut at the time. Its stated aim was to protect Lebanese civilians from the radical Muslims and the PLO. Its actual activities, in concert with the Israeli military, helped to heighten tensions and violence.

Members of the Free Lebanon Army worked as night guards, watching over the safety of the people. My involvement with the military activities of the Christian-sponsored elements of the civil war began with my clandestine support of nighttime patrols and watches. Many nights I would sneak out of the house and join my friends on guard duty. My parents had forbidden me from accompanying them, but I was intent on doing this and went secretly. I wanted to prove to everyone and to myself that I was able to carry a weapon. I did not have my own gun, but some nights I took the place of my friends on duty when they were very tired. I remember the first time I got to do this. My eyes were open wide as saucers, watching for intruders or any sort of movement. My ears were keenly alert to any suspicious sound. Using their gun, my sweaty hands held the weapon tightly, ready to shoot. I heard many noises I had never heard before! My fear was that they would suddenly surprise me and shoot me before I could even respond. I did a good job and felt that I was fulfilling something of the responsibilities of a first-born son. I proved to my leaders and to all of my friends that I was capable of defending my village just as well as any of the other brave men. My reward for this work was a pack of cigarettes every night.

It was important to my ego to prove to my family, and my friends that I was brave and strong. Becoming a part of the FLA gave me the opportunity to join in the work of defending my village, the region, and my country. It is very accurate to say that in the coming years, my willingness to go to war, even if it would be necessary to sacrifice my life in battle, was the outworking of my sense of cultural responsibility to family and country. I was so proud of myself for what I was doing. I was participating in an organization whose purpose was to free my nation from PLO terror and the occupation of other countries and parties such as Hezbala that were using Lebanon for their own purposes that had nothing to do with the good of Lebanon. In this effort we worked closely with the Israeli Defense Force (IDF). I lied to my parents about going out in the evenings. I did not want them to know what I was doing. I especially hid this from my father who was very hard on me at that time. I even thought of ways to leave the house and get out from under his control. I didn't know that my father actually knew everything that was happening, but held his peace.

Although I was still a student working toward my high school diploma, I had by now become a fully engaged participant in the civil war of Lebanon. Angry with the people and causes that had brought death and destruction to my beloved homeland, seeking to meet my obligations as oldest son, I had been forced by circumstances to take sides in a war I never wanted. My personal life and character suffered greatly as I struggled to understand the life fate had given to me. There were many internal struggles as I tried to figure out and resolve the conditions into which my family and friends had devolved. The phony maturity of military life coupled with the natural inclinations to all sorts of carnal pleasures left my conscience in such a turmoil that I finally even wanted to give up on life. In some ways, death would have been a welcome escape from the inward and outward struggles I was facing.

I boldly progressed in my military service to take the very front row of the army. I wanted to appear courageous and that is just how most of my peers came to see me. I was eager to serve as an example to others, to demonstrate by deeds that ours was a cause to believe in. This was in fact just my way of concealing a growing fatalistic attitude toward life, an almost casual disregard for my life since it seemed that I had nothing for which to live. Facing death for the sake of my village and family was the best solution I could think of. I was desperate and empty inside, full of darkness and pessimism. In the military, I confronted death every night and I often wondered why I didn't get hit. I was living in youthful naïveté according to an old Lebanese saying, "Attack death and death will flee." Many times bombs exploded near me; bullets shot just over my head or near my legs and side. Not once was I struck. Many times I faced enemies who were shooting at me, but missed. Three times my friends accidentally directed their guns at me and shot, but missed. Other times we would get into arguments with knives, but never was I seriously wounded.

There were other times when I barely escaped death. I crossed a field to get a little closer to the enemy. I took a step over a trench when my foot landed about one centimeter away from a landmine. I was not expecting landmines in that field. I tried to stand still, but I was shaking with fear, not able to move either of my feet. I knew that if I made one small mistake the landmine would explode. I held my leg in one position to stabilize it in its place and started shouting to my friends to help me. I avoided injury that time and escaped possible death.

Just living at home was dangerous. Our village was bombed daily. Sometimes it was in the morning and at other times in the afternoon and during the night. There was nothing predictable about it. Sitting in the living room with the whole family, we heard a big explosion as a bomb landed in my parents' bedroom! The pressure from the explosion threw me about ten feet from where I had been sitting. Everyone was screaming and my sisters were crying. The dust and smoke from the explosion obscured our vision and at first I couldn't tell if anyone was injured. I heard my mother calling out our names to see if we were hurt or even worse. Miraculously, no one was injured. My mother quickly took us to one corner of the bathroom, the safest place in our home. The shelling continued and bombs were falling all around our house, throughout our neighborhood. We waited for a period of silence and then ran to my grandfather's house were there was a bomb shelter. We sat there, peering at each other, feeling terrified and helpless. We stayed in the shelter all night, not knowing if we would be attacked again. We were able to go back home in the morning when everything was safe and quiet. After that attack, we often slept in the shelter and we would run there every time there was bombing. We often changed shelters if the bombing intensified in a certain area. The lower the level of the shelter, the safer it was. After some time, we were able to determine the source of the bomb, its size, and approximately where it would explode. Wherever we were, we would lie down with out faces to the floor and cover our heads for protection when we heard cannon fire.

There are many painful memories of the death and destruction that became a way of life for us Christians in Lebanon. One of the more painful and gruesome events for me had to do with the meager medical care that was available in our small village. Because of the large number of injuries from the fighting, I volunteered to help the few village doctors at the clinic. Sadly, the first people I saw killed were the village doctor and his assistant. I saw them lying on the floor in the examination room. I was shocked and frightened. Their bodies were covered with blood. My hands were shaking as I helped the nurses fill up the holes in the corpses and wipe off the blood. I could make no sense why a kind and helpful person like this doctor had to die, but there was no time to think about it or for questions. I had to help the wounded and comfort them.

Another incident, among the many that solidified my deep anger and determination to fight back against my enemies, occurred when some terrorists attached an explosive booby trap to my uncle's house. His house was right next door to our own and because he was an officer in the SLA, he occasionally hosted military leadership meetings. Early one evening there was a loud explosion followed by the loud screams of a woman. My mother would not allow me to leave the house and even locked the door in an attempt to keep me from the obvious dangers outside. The continued screams finally prompted me to jump out a window. As I approached my uncle's house I found that no one was there. They had all left earlier for the bomb shelter. As I began to walk away, I heard groans and a pathetic cry for help coming from the back yard. When I aimed my flashlight in the direction of the moaning sounds, I saw my best friend's brother-in-law hanging from the branch of a lemon tree, nearly torn in two at the waist. He pleaded, "Help me ... hospital ... !" I tried to calm him when I heard another voice, a woman, also pleading for help. As I turned to look, I realized it was this man's sister-in-law. I told them I would get help. I ran a great distance barefoot, looking for someone who could help. At last I found another man who asked why I was screaming for help. When I realized that the injured people were his wife and brother, I continued to run, looking for someone else to help. Finally I found help, but by the time we returned, we discovered that others were already helping the injured. There was no possibility that these two could survive such terrible trauma. Others died or were wounded, including children, in this cruel and clandestine act of terror.

By the time I returned home at the end of the next day, my feelings of anger were intense. I wanted to kill in revenge. In my bitterness of heart I even inwardly challenged God's goodness and justice in allowing such tragedies to occur. And so I was compelled to become personally involved in Lebanon's civil war and the broader conflict. I found my place among the Rightists who were the ethnic and religious parties that resented the radical agendas of those who hated Israel. Our enemies were the leftists who formed the ethnic and religious parties whose commitment and *raison d'etre* was principally the destruction of the hated Jews and their nation of Israel. In taking sides I was only following the heritage of my birth and upbringing. The terror techniques of the enemy seemed especially loathsome, but in fighting the fire, it seemed that a firestorm was also smoldering in my own soul. Hopelessness and despair were finding their place in my heart alongside of the anger and bitterness toward the enemy. Military life is not wholesome for a teenage boy and I was rapidly sinking into a moral and ethical pit from which I could see no escape. I had become a walking dead man. All of my youthful hopes and dreams had now vanished in a civil war of killings and misery all about me. My favored position in our family now burdened me with responsibilities that I could not fulfill under the circumstances. My lifeless and cultural Christian faith had not prepared me with the character that would be required in facing enemies and warfare. I was a soldier, filled with hate and ready to kill. I was living in a military environment that was self-serving and immoral. I did not see the pathway of God before me. Not only did I hate my enemies, but now I was frustrated with God, as well. I angrily asked why He allowed such things to happen to us?

Elie during the Lebanese civil war

My involvement in the war and military activities grew rapidly. I was sent to Israel for training and my enthusiastic and passionate participation caught the eye of Israeli leaders. I loved the tasks given to me and those over me were eager to promote me and advance my career in helping them to secure the buffer zone to the north of their country. In so many ways, my life as a soldier was filled with poor choices and an immoral lifestyle. The volunteer guard duty that had started as a youthful thrill to prove my manhood, rewarded with a pack of cigarettes, now became the serious duty of protecting our village and the security zone in the south controlled by Israel in South Lebanon, rewarded with even more grown-up vices. Every night I helped in guard duty I would get my free cigarettes and some pocket money, which I usually spent on alcohol and more cigarettes. Smoking and drinking led me to other related poor choices. I started going to gambling places and playing poker. Eventually I started to earn big money. I found that earning money in the wrong way wasn't so hard after all. Every time I got paid a tidy sum, I headed out to gamble. I would spend up to seven hours playing on poker machines until I lost every penny of the money. I would get so mad that I would kick the machine and break it. I wanted to kill the owner once because I was so angry at having lost two months' salary. I left the place not knowing where to go. How could I go home? Everyone was expecting me to come home with the money. It was Christmas time and I had promised to get gifts for everyone in the family. Now I had nothing; I had lost it all at the poker machine.

I remember thinking that killing myself was the only solution. I could not face my predicament. My thoughts were evil. I even considered killing someone and stealing his money. I went down a quiet alley, holding my rifle, and sat there waiting for a car to pass by. My plan was to stop the car, kill the driver, and steal his money. Two hours passed and no cars went by. Finally, I dragged myself home. I entered the house smelling of alcohol. Sullen and in despair, I spoke to no one and went directly to bed. I slept that night hoping that I would not wake up the next day. But the next morning did arrive for me. I left the house without talking to anyone. I headed to the house of a friend and borrowed money from him. I went to stores and bought the promised gifts. No one knew what had happened; no one but God and myself.

My addiction to gambling grew with the days. I wanted to replace all the money I had lost, but I kept losing more.

I resorted to heavy drinking and smoking just to forget my troubles. I even started using hashish. The harder I tried to run from my reality, the deeper I sank with my addictions. The sad thing was that I wanted someone to help me and comfort me, but none of my friends could do anything for me. We were all alike. We were all drowning in the same filthy pit. At the very time when I most desperately needed supernatural help, I turned to evil spiritual forces and never thought to turn to God Himself. I turned again to the occult. Seeking guidance and comfort, I went with some relatives to another fortuneteller. This man was considered the best. I entered the room and felt the same pressure and fear as I had before. Smoky incense filled the room, pictures of saints, and candles. It was said that this fortuneteller could speak 15 languages with *al-'afarit* angels. He started to speak with these spirits in many languages that no one could understand, calling them by strange names in prayers. After a while he started to tell us what they were saying to him about us. They knew which village we were from, some things about our past, and why we had come, but they did not know our future. He became tired after telling us what he knew and we heard him command the spirits that we couldn't see, "Go now, I cannot tolerate you." Then he started to shout at them to leave him. He closed a book in front of him and told us that he could not speak with them more than 30 minutes because they are strong and if he would keep them, they might control and kill him.

But God Himself had been watching and caring about the agony and emptiness I felt. Even though I did not know enough to seek him, he would graciously be the initiator and seek me out.

Chapter 6
Life After Death

My anger had led me to military involvement. I harbored a sense of purpose in fighting the enemy, but the inner turmoil was not resolved. God would deal with that.

My life had become a downward spiral of death and destruction. What had started out only a few years before as the confusion and fear of a young boy watching his homeland collapse into civil war had now become the anger and violence of a young man's participation in actual military operations. This pathetic progression was an inward battle and personal tragedy because I was without God and without hope. In a strange way my desires were sincere and simple. I merely wanted to protect and preserve the lives and homes of my family and friends in our Christian village. My argument was with the radical Palestinians who were bent on destroying Lebanon if necessary in their fight with Israel. I strongly believed that I was just being a good Catholic Christian and that the fanatic Muslims and other groups on the left were my enemies. It was justice for which I was fighting. Although I had many friends within the camaraderie of the military, I knew that my heart was empty, except for the anger and hatred of my enemies. I continued to satisfy myself and numb my conscience with heavy drinking and hashish. Each time I would wake in the morning after a night of binging, my heart was full of fear and pain. Many times I wondered how I could change the way I was living and become a totally different person, but I did not know how to do it. So I continued to serve in the army. The smell of death was all about me, physically and spiritually.

By 1982, I was finally completing my studies to receive my senior high school diploma and, as usual, was facing hard times at school. Although still a student, I had been officially a part of the SLA since 1978. I drove military cars to school, parked them outside the school campus, and attended classes wearing my military uniform. I don't know how I made it through that year, but I remember being very pleased and satisfied with the grades I received at the year's end. Actually I barely passed, but I did not mind passing with poor grades. My goal was simply to pass. I wasn't like my classmates who pursued higher grades. I could see their faces light up when they received their report cards. I had what I considered more important matters on my mind. I was working to save my country, but I was also longing secretly for answers to the bigger questions about life and about God.

My original participation in night watchman duties with the FLA had grown over the years to full time service in the SLA. I was sent to Israel for more advanced training with the result that I became a leader in the Lebanese military cooperation with Israel in our efforts to secure the buffer zone in the south of Lebanon from the Hezbollah and other terrorist activities of Israel. Back in Lebanon, I was put in charge of securing what was known as checkpoint "K" between the Bekaa Valley and the buffer zone. We were under attack almost daily and many of the SLA soldiers died in our efforts to protect the civilian populations from terrorism. The viciousness and lack of human compassion which are the *modus operandi* of terrorists are very difficult for the soldier to combat. It was all but impossible to know where and when a religiously motivated killer would strike.

Israeli forces invaded Lebanon once again in 1982, this time reaching as far as Beirut in their attempt to root out the PLO military power in southern Lebanon and to improve their security zone there. The result of this invasion was the flight of the PLO to Tunis, Tunisia. A UN multinational force worked to protect the remaining Palestinian civilians. French and US forces sought to quell the Lebanese civil war. But when the Israelis finally withdrew from Lebanon, it was the South Lebanon Army (SLA), of which I was by now a member, that was assigned the difficult task of working with the Israeli military to provide a security buffer zone on her northern border. My responsibility expanded. I was an ally of Israel and deeply involved with the Christian faction in the civil war of Lebanon. My life was getting more and more out of control as I became deeply involved in the Middle East struggles. While I felt a strong sense of purpose in what I was doing, the stresses of this life were taking their toll as I struggled with my enemies and the God who seemed to ignore my questions.

But God had not forsaken me. Although I had made a shambles of my own life, He heard the cry of my heart for real peace. He showed compassion in spite of my ignorance, my selfishness, and my hate. He was merciful toward my blindness as I responded badly to all the struggles surrounding my circumstances and the battles within me. He was in the process of opening another option for me. Little did I know to what lengths He would go to bring me to choose another way.

In the early 1980's, as the civil war intensified, some missionaries from the west came to my region and began to share a gospel of Jesus Christ as Savior, very different from the teachings of the cultural and political Christianity with which I grew up. This outreach was a part of the work of the Voice of Hope Ministries and radio network founded by George Otis, Sr. The message was that Jesus can give rest, peace, and eternal life to the ones who believe in him and confess their sins, surrendering their lives to Him. The message of these missionaries presented a personal relationship with God through Jesus Christ, a message that had not been given a clear voice before within the cultural Christianity of this region. Major Saad Haddad, the leader of the South Lebanese Army, had already become an evangelical Christian and now the entire region was hearing the gospel in a fresh and lively way from these missionaries and the radio station that they built just outside our village. Many in the area were desperate for good news. So the Word was received and many believed. Little groups of lively Christians began to meet in house churches and soon were renting a facility for regular group meetings. Three of my five sisters received Jesus as their Savior and were converted to this living and personal brand of the faith. This made me quite angry, especially when they started attending the meetings of this Christian group. I was especially angry that they no longer went to the Catholic Church. In my anger, I made attempts to put a halt to these meetings.

My sisters began to share the gospel with me and told me what had happened to them; how their lives had been changed. I thought that the people they had joined were bad people and I did what I could to stop my sisters from being part of this group. I used a nice way at first and gentle words to try to convince them not to go any more. But it didn't work. Everything I said about us being the real Christians and all our fighting for our beliefs did not help either. They loved going to these meetings. I had never seen them happier in my life, but I was not convinced. I used my authority as their big brother. I hid their bibles and watched them carefully to see if they would try to go to the meetings even though I forbade them to do so. Many times I entered the places where they had the meetings and destroyed them. Even my parents encouraged me to do this. My father burned all the books they had that contained this "new" evangelical Christian doctrine.

Whatever way we tried to stop them, however, failed; their faith was growing stronger. Somehow I knew that they had begun to pray for me. They secretly put a Bible in my car and another one under my pillow. I had to admit that I was curious to know what the Bible contained and I wanted to read it without anyone finding out about it. I did not know what parts to read or even where to start. Whenever I was on duty in the service, I would open the Bible and try to read it, but I understood nothing of what I read. Many times fear would overcome me and I had to discontinue reading and close the book.

I had seen changes in my sisters' lives and the lives of other people in their group. They seemed to have what I had been searching for a long time. They were happy and peaceful people. I was actually jealous of them. What was happening to me? I remember having a great desire to pray that seemed to come up out of nowhere, but I still did not know how. I even wanted to attend their meetings but knew I couldn't. My pride and fear prevented me from doing anything religious. I feared other people's opinions and especially the views of my friends. What would they think of me if they knew that I had started attending these religious meetings? They all knew that I was a big sinner; they knew all my evil actions. How would they ever believe that I saw a need to change?

Despite all my pride and fear, the hunger I felt within me and the joy I saw in the lives of my sisters and others who had found this new Christianity caused me to look further into their new faith. I began to make many attempts to attend the meetings. I would park my car far from the church and pretend to be going to a friend's house. As soon as someone saw me, I would change my direction. If I entered the meeting room, I would sit in the back, trying to hide my face and then leave quickly without anyone noticing me. One time I went and surprised the people in the church. In the past, I had only attended church for funerals or weddings. That day all eyes gazed at me with a look that mixed wonder and fear. I remember thinking that the prayers, songs, and even the sermon were all focusing on me. I wanted to leave but something kept me fixed to my seat. When the meeting was over, I was the first one to leave. I didn't want anyone to speak to me, but one of the leaders was standing at the door waiting to greet me. He expressed his happiness to see me and told me that I was welcome anytime. I tried to brush past him, but someone else came to talk to me. And then a group of people gathered around me, all expressing with big smiles their pleasure at seeing me. Slowly I withdrew and, once outside, ran to my car. I could not wait to light a cigarette, and I drove off speeding down the road while making the decision never to go back there again. I could not stop thinking about the subject of the sermon. "The believer who shines like a star … ." The preacher had encouraged the believers to share the light of Jesus Christ in their lives to those around them. "What could that mean," I thought, "to shine like a star?" We were at war; our lives suffered daily; enemies were overpowering us. How could these people be so happy, so content, so unafraid…so forgiving?

God was closing in on Elie Hasbani. Inwardly, there was a great war going on as I struggled with a conflicting conscience. I knew that the life I was living could not be pleasing to God. I was frustrated at being caught up in the failure of my fellow countrymen to put aside religious and partisan hatreds. I had longed to have answers, to understand, to be cleansed; even to be loved and accepted. Now at last I sensed that there was an answer to all my questions, a satisfaction for that inner emptiness, and a fulfillment to all of my desires, but I could also see that this would require me to forsake all that life had become to me. As I continued to wrestle with this internal conflict, God brought me to my moment of decision. I could now see that there were two different worlds: one world was filled with hatred and war, the world I was living in so painfully and with so much disappointment and failure; the other world was filled with peace and joy, the world that beckoned me to sit in heavenly places with King Jesus.

On October 10, 1985, I received an order from the General Command to take my troops and go to enemy territory on a mission to destroy some rockets that were aimed at our position. So my friends and I took our guns and headed toward the area where the rockets were suspected to be. On our way there, I was supposed to be very cautious and ready for any surprise from the enemy. I had to be in constant contact with the General Command by way of walkie-talkie. Our mission was to find and disable the rockets before they could be launched against our positions or into some village of innocent civilians.

We got out of our vehicles and I gave instructions on how to reach the spot on Mount Abu Kamha, under the Mount of Hermon, where the rockets were suspected to be. Cautiously, we started hiking to reach the top of this mountain. Suddenly we found three rockets! As soon as I spotted them I contacted my leader and informed him that the first part of our mission was completed. Then he gave me the order to disable the rockets before they could be set off.

I looked at my friends, made the sign of the cross over my face, and stepped forward to accomplish the mission. The rockets were connected with wires to a stopwatch and were set to detonate in fifteen minutes. I had to act quickly, but carefully. I had to find the correct wire to cut in order to disable them. My friend handed me a pair of pliers that were rather blunt and difficult to use. I was so scared something would go wrong and that the rockets would explode. As the leader, though, I had to do it. I carefully considered which wire to cut. Fortunately, it was the one that disabled the rockets.

I stepped back and said to my friends, "I did it!" They were all sweating from exhaustion and fear. We were relieved, but still had one thing to do: change the direction of the rockets for more safety. So I asked my friends to keep watch, guarding while I changed their direction. I moved the first one, then the second, and finally the third. I was kneeling down at the time. As I stood up, the earth exploded under me. The force and power of the explosion lifted me high into the air and I landed on the ground on my back and hands. I lay there like a dirty, discarded, limp rag. I could not comprehend what had happened. I smelled something burning only to realize it was my own flesh. The taste of blood and dirt filled my mouth. I thought that one of the rockets had exploded or that the enemy had attacked. Then I felt the pain. A terrible pain wracked my whole body. Before looking in the direction of the pain, I started to lose it. I felt like I was torn to pieces. I tried to lift myself up to a standing position, but I couldn't.

Suddenly, the thought came to me that I was going to die. This time I was dying for real. I was so scared! What would happen when I died? I was sure I was going to hell. What could I do? I tried to hold my breath inside of me, thinking that my spirit was about to come out of me. I started to pray for the comfort of my parents and friends. Desperate and frightened, I lifted up my head and gazed into the sky. Up in the heavens I saw a small cloud. Then the thought occurred to me, "My only hope is Jesus." Even though I believed in saints, I knew that they could not save me now. I shouted with all my strength, "Jesus, I know you are alive and I know you are true. Please save me and take me to heaven. I don't want to go to hell. Forgive all my sins. I am a big sinner. I don't want to die." I was trying to hold onto life even though I had often wished for death. I realized at that moment how important and precious life is, at the very moment I was about to lose it. I continued to pray to Jesus, "If you save me and keep me alive, I will be yours forever. I will serve you and follow you and tell everyone about you."

As soon as I finished my prayer, I heard a voice like a wind coming from heaven. It came on me and I felt peaceful, happy both in my body and in my soul. A strange power filled me; I started to laugh and praise God out loud. What was happening to me? I had changed in a second! I tried to sit up and this time I did it very easily. I looked at my body, covered with blood. I saw my left leg completely burned and hanging on the skin. The bone had been completely broken and crushed. My other leg was bleeding and my calf was cut severely. I started yelling, "My leg is gone! My leg is gone! But I am still alive! Thank you, God. Thank you, Jesus."

I had been a walking dead man, lost in selfish confusion and bitter hatred. My life had gone wrong in every way. Now I had passed from death to life. Walking in my body would now be difficult the rest of my life, but I had come alive and would now be able to walk with God.

PART III
LOVE CHANGES

Chapter 7
Suffering and Love

A crisis had precipitated my decision to follow God in a new way. The months ahead would be the experience of enjoying the God's great love and discovering how it would change my life.

God has a way of charging into our lives; when He does, our first reaction is often a joyous submission to whatever circumstances and struggles He has used to bring us to that change point. This was my reaction. The landmine catastrophe was about to rob me of my left leg, but it had brought about my decision to follow Jesus. In one horrifying moment, the great internal conflict I had endured was resolved. I struggled with the misery in the world around me and all the ways it had changed my life and my relationships. I had been fighting for my country, my religion, and a way of life to which I felt entitled, but all the time I knew there was something wrong. I had longed for something better and truly meaningful. The "new" life that my sisters had discovered seemed to provide them the inner satisfaction I was seeking. Then, in that fiery moment, I had made a decision. I had gladly accepted the gracious offer of salvation Jesus made to me, but there would follow a season of learning to hear and obey, to submit to the voice of the master peacemaker.

In the moments immediately following the explosion and the miracle of my salvation, I realized that the bleeding from my leg was a life-threatening danger. I had a rope with me and used it to tie a tourniquet around my leg. I shouted to my friends who thought the enemy had attacked and I was dead. They were wildly shooting in every direction and were surprised to hear my voice. Rushing to my aid, they tied my leg still tighter; I had not been able to stop the bleeding on my own. We continued to be on guard for the enemy, but realized they weren't the source of the explosion nor was it the rockets I was working to defuse. I had been standing on a land mine the whole time and it exploded right under me. My friends thought I had gone crazy because they had heard me laughing and now saw that I was smiling. One of them said, "He must have fallen on his head and damaged his brain!" I tried to convince them I wasn't crazy, but they did not understand the amazing change that had taken place in me after the explosion.

Once my leg had been secured as best they could, my friends quickly called the high command and asked for an ambulance and medical aid, but first they had to carry me to the bottom of the mountain, a long, one hour descent. They tried to hold my shattered leg in place as we made our way down. I was in severe pain and it became worse as the minutes passed. Every step of the way down was very dangerous. One wrong move could lead to more trouble and even cost us our lives. The men carrying me had to follow the steps of one leader who carefully chose rocks to step on. It was a terrifying and strenuous process for them and they were exhausted by the time we reached the bottom. I could easily have died from all the bleeding. During this time, despite all the pain, a strange peace filled me and I was very calm. Finally, the treacherous descent came to an end and an ambulance was waiting for us. They rushed me to the nearest hospital for treatment. I was immediately given an injection to fight infection. My face was so bloodied, burned, cut, and covered with dirt, that nurses I knew personally did not even recognize me. The whole time we were making our way to the hospital, they tried to keep me conscious, but now I found myself drifting off as I headed into the operating room.

When I woke up after the operation, I was lying on a bed, covered with a white sheet. I could feel the pain in my legs. I uncovered myself only to see my left leg had been cut off below the knee. They could not save it. Accepting this truth was a great challenge. I was not prepared emotionally to cope with the reality of the loss and I started sobbing. My family was there, gathered around me…all of them crying. They tried to comfort me, but it was no use. The pain was severe since the anesthetic had now worn off. One of my sisters, a nurse at the hospital, gave me some painkillers, but at that moment, nothing could numb the pain of my new reality.

I was in the hospital for more than a month. My room never seemed empty of family and friends. Gratefully, I remember the camaraderie I had with those who served with me in the SLA, both my friends and superiors. These men did not abandon me at all. Indeed, they shared in my pain and sorrow, visiting me often and sincerely grieving with me over the loss of my leg and the impact it would have on my life. General Lahad of the SLA and General Youda of the IDF made personal visits to my hospital room. I received medals of honor, for service and courage. They honored me with their tears over what I was going through. I never had any reason to feel abandoned in my circumstances. The financial and medical help did not cease; and the encouragement from my friends and family continued.

During my hospital stay, I began to tell others of my experience on the mountain. I started to tell my story to the friends who had thought I was crazy because I was laughing on the mountain. I talked of what had transpired between God and myself up there, in that moment when I lost my leg, but my life had been spared and found, all at the same time. Christians heard of my experience and began to gather around me. They were a great source of support and encouragement. They prayed daily with me and we often had Bible discussions in my room. During this time in the hospital, I began again to read the Bible I had been given. I had often been confused and frightened by what I read, but now, I was able to understand. The missionaries who were in the area visited me regularly. I shared with them the experience of feeling peace during the explosion and that I really didn't understand why. Maybe my friends were correct and I was crazy! They described what I had felt as the power of the Holy Spirit, the Comforter, whom Jesus sent to help support me and give me rest.

I continued to have opportunity to share my story, my encounter with the living God, while I was in the hospital and after I had returned home. My new found brothers and sisters in Jesus took time to encourage and counsel me in my new faith. My family was a source of strength and I could always count on them as they reassured me things would get better; even though they, too, grieved my lost leg. Three of my sisters were a very special support spiritually during all of this time. Georgette, Joumana, and Diana were older than me in the Lord. I could always count on them to be an encouragement when I was discouraged. They offered spiritual words of wisdom that reassured me of God's love when the road to peace with God, this road of new found faith, seemed rough.

I often worried about my future, especially when I was alone, struggling with my doubt-filled questions of what would come. Why was I going through all of this? Why the unbearable pain? How could I live with only one leg? What would people think of me? The questions were continually in my thoughts as I began to rebuild my life. I needed resources for care and rehabilitation. In Lebanon, as in much of the third world, there are no laws to protect the disabled. The handicapped have no consideration with regard to health care, education, employment, recreational activities, transportation, as exists in the West. I felt like a second-class citizen, rejected and without value. How could I survive this? I became more dependent on other people than I had ever been or wanted to be. I recognized that I not only needed physical help; I needed help emotionally, mentally, and socially. The loss of my leg damaged all areas of my life.

The 'why' questions became profoundly painful and even challenging toward God. Was I suffering now because I had rejected him earlier, refusing to believe in Him? If so, can God really be that cruel? Wasn't he good? I found myself blaming God many time for everything. I accepted my situation even though deep down within me, I did not. Could this be love? I prayed often and hard. I searched the

Scriptures for answers. I knew I was being prayed for and loved by my sisters and my new Christian friends. This helped me to hold firmly to the joy I found in my new faith. I found I experienced more of his peace and comfort within my circumstances as I learned to trust the Lord Jesus.

My Christian friends taught me that the Bible states the Lord disciplines the ones He loves. I wasn't sure I liked what they were telling me. They pointed me to Paul's similar struggles with his 'thorn in the flesh,' through which he learned that God's grace is sufficient, indeed, that God's very strength is perfected when we are the weakest. They often added my name to the verses they read to me, making it a very personal application of the truth to my life. Sometimes it made me wonder, though, if I were a bigger sinner than any of them because it was me who was suffering. Did God love them more than me? I respected their knowledge of God's Word and had to believe that God continued to love me through all my pain. I had to embrace his design for my life and accept that in this fallen, sinful world, God is not to be faulted. I was taking small steps to secure my peace with God. I needed wisdom from above and humility to learn as I continued my walk with Jesus.

Sitting in my hospital room, I asked the Lord to help me look beyond my own situation. I began to see that people throughout the world struggled daily in a condition of pain; in a world full of hurt that seems to serve no purpose. I thought of people who must struggle merely to feed and shelter their families; to come to terms with the loss of a loved one; or to stand under the weight of a terrible illness. Rather than lifting my eyes to heaven and demanding an answer to 'Why me, God?', I began to understand that each of us suffers personally in a way no one else can fully understand. My nation, my family and friends, even my new church family had suffered in some way through no fault of their own. A war, an accident, a birth defect…these are the cold facts of life. I wondered why God hadn't created a world where nothing would ever go wrong? Couldn't he have made a world where people would never have the ability to make bad choices? I knew that he could have, but He didn't.

We do try to figure God out. We have a picture or certain ideas about God that we keep feeding until we believe our ideas are correct. Some have come to feel he is very distant and cruel at heart, punishing sinners and people who refuse him. He keeps watching people and when they do something wrong, he hurts them. I grew up hearing these ideas about God, both in church and from my own parents. God was used to scare children so they wouldn't do bad things. I saw many contradictions even with those who said they had faith, people who tried to please God by torturing their own bodies in order to show their love for God. Good deeds were done to avoid the guilt they felt due to the bad things they had done. In each case, I came to believe that they, too, were looking for peace with God in their own way.

Like so many before me, I struggled with these thoughts in the lonely hours in the hospital and later when I returned home. Painful questions over the existence of good and evil in the world kept me awake. I wasn't looking for just answers. I wanted the inner turmoil I had experienced for so long to end. I began to have some understand as I studied God's Word, the Bible. I learned that our first parents, Adam and Eve, had made a very poor decision when tempted by Satan in the Garden of Eden. The consequences of that decision destroyed the tranquility of their existence and passed on to us the pain of living in a world changed by sin. God gave his creation free will to choose with the risk of choosing wrong over right. I learned as I matured in my new faith that a sovereign, and holy God could be trusted to walk with us through all the pain of a world full of sin. I began to find the rest I had sought for so long. I was convinced of his love for me so I was willing to yield to his lordship in my life, trusting that his understanding of the events in this world was far beyond mine.

God graciously revealed truth to me through his Word as I studied it. Paul's words in Romans 8:14-18 seemed to leap from the pages into my heart and mind.

> Those who are led by the Spirit of God are sons of God. For you did not receive a spirit that makes you a slave again to fear, but you received the Spirit who makes you sons. And by him we cry, 'Abba, Father.'

> The Spirit himself testifies with our spirit that we are God's children. Now if we are children, then we are heirs, heirs of God and co-heirs with Christ, if indeed we share in his sufferings in order that we may also share in his glory, I consider that our present sufferings are not worth comparing with the glory that will be revealed in us. (NIV)

Suffering with him brings eternal glory. God showed me that there is a difference in pain for the sake of the Lord or endured with the Lord. I came to see that it is not God who brings pain to individuals, but rather that pain comes from Satan and our own wrong choices, leading to sin.

I began to see God's gracious hand in my life and those around me as I endured the long weeks of recovery in the hospital. The bombings in and around the villages continued mercilessly. The dangers were great and we could never be sure of our safety. My sister, Georgette, worked as an announcer at the *Voice of Hope* Christian radio station, located just outside of our village. She was scheduled to be at the station one day, but because she also cared for me in the hospital, she changed her schedule and was with me. While she was gone from the radio station, a group of terrorists attacked. They killed the guards and then went on to kill all those working there. The station building was then blown up. My sister was spared.

When I no longer needed hospital care, I returned home to begin learning how to function as a handicapped person. Moving about was difficult and humbling as I needed to accept help for even the most simple of tasks. I either used crutches or had to lean on someone in the family in order to walk anywhere. It took me a long time to adapt to the loss of my leg and the pain continued. I felt weak and useless most of the time. It sounds strange, but I often would forget my leg was no longer there and would try to stand, only to fall down. Stairs were the most difficult to maneuver. Not long after I came home, I fell coming down the stairs and broke a bone in my leg. I was crushed to hear from the doctor that I would have to go through another operation. I was assured that it would be a comparatively simple procedure. I had no choice but to have the surgery so I prayed, asking Jesus to take care of me.

In the operating room, I remember the anesthetic beginning to have its effect. The nurse wished me good luck, but I sensed myself hanging in midair. I looked down and saw the earth beneath me. I looked up and saw the throne of God. But then a spiritual battle began to take place. It was as though Satan began to attack me and beat me with a stick. As I called out the name of Jesus, Satan's anger only increased against me and he vowed that God would not save me so I should stop calling out in *that* Name. In a flight of fancy, I found refuge in a large trumpet. As I entered the horn, retreating into the mechanism of the valves, beautiful notes began to sound. This dream has become a beautiful picture for me of God's great power and wisdom to confront the terrible attacks that Satan causes.

Who ho shall separate us from the love of Christ? Shall trouble or hardship or persecution or famine or nakedness or danger or sword?

> As it is written: 'For your sake we face death all the day long; we are considered as sheep to be slaughtered.' No, in all these things we are more than conquerors through him who loved us. For I am convinced that neither death nor life, neither angels nor demons, neither the present nor the future, nor any powers, neither height nor depth, nor anything else in all creation will be able to separate us from the love of God that is in Christ Jesus our Lord. -Romans 8:35-39 (NIV)

Paul's words in the New Testament again played in my head during this dream state. I was learning that even Satan's attacks could be turned to bring glory to God; to be used for his purposes of *the* good in my life and those who trust in him.

I woke up suddenly after the operation had been completed. The pain was so intense. I was still in the fog that comes with being under an anesthetic and I found I could not explain the pain I was in. I cried out for Jesus to help me and it came in the form of morphine. When the nurse came to give me the injection, it was discovered that the stitches in my leg had come undone. I had lost so much blood that a transfusion was needed, leading to a near fatal reaction. I was given the wrong blood type. The doctor later told me he had never seen anything like it before and didn't really understand all that had happened.

But I knew. This was a spiritual battle. I was in a battle not only for my physical well-being, but also for my very soul. I remembered the times I had ignorantly sought Satan's help in my life by going to fortune-tellers. Although, at the time, I had no idea what I had done during my times of despair, I had actually opened corners of my life to him. Would I seek Jesus and be for him; or would I side with his enemy? That was the heart of the battle. Satan had waged a battle with me because I now belonged to the kingdom of God; I had turned toward him, having a relationship with him through the Lord Jesus. Satan was angered by my change of allegiance and would rather kill me than allow me to side with God. Once again, Jesus saved me from death: the first time from eternal death, eternal separation from his presence, as I was lying injured on the ground; and now he had saved me from physical death as I entered into a lifetime of battle with the enemy of God.

A tragedy brought me into a relationship with Jesus. There were times after I lost my leg that the enemy of

God caused me to question the goodness of God and even his integrity. The Holy Spirit of God, given to those who come into a relationship with Jesus, used my study of the Scriptures and the guidance of my new Christian friends to teach me and strengthen me for this battle. I was learning to trust God's ultimate wisdom for my life rather that question him. I had found a wonderful peace with God.

The experience of confidently submitting all my life's pain and loss to be swallowed up in the love of God brought joyful tears. My pillow was drenched with them one night when this time, Jesus came to me in a dream. My room was filled with a bright light. I saw myself in heaven had an indescribable sense of happiness. I was stepping on long grass that had life. It didn't break and die when I walked on it. Instead, it grew up instantly and took its former shape. Then I saw my leg growing until it became perfect once again. I knew at that moment the One who could renew every blade of grass would one day remake and perfect my leg. It was an incredible vision that filled me with joy. I woke up with a strange feeling that my leg was still there. I opened my Bible and a verse lit up before my eyes: "I will never leave you nor forsake you." I closed the Bible and opened it again. The same verse appeared to me! Jesus was talking to me, planting a new hope in my heart. God was preparing an eternal body for me that would never die or have the possibility of being disabled again. That's part of the hope we have in Christ for life after death. Yes, I had lost my leg, but I now had eternal life! Matthew 5:30 became very personal for me: "It is better for you to lose one part of your body than for your whole body to go to hell." I was convinced God was making everything work for *the* good in my life.

The peace of God continued to hedge me in more tightly as my faith became the dominant piece in my life. I began to see all the experiences of my life being brought together as important pieces of my calling from God. "I shall not die, but live, and *declare* the works of the Lord. The Lord chastened me severely, but he had not given me over to death." (Psalm 118:17, KJV) This verse became *my* verse. I renewed the decision I had made when I was lying on the ground dying after the land mine explosion. I made a firm decision to follow and serve him the rest of my life. What had appeared to be a great loss had truly become the pathway to great gain. The driving desire of my life from that point on was to become nothing less than a follower, a disciple of Jesus Christ. I didn't want to become a 'religious man' or a priest or a pastor, as I had known them in my youth. I wanted simply to know and to do the will of God, to be like Jesus.

To know the will of God for my life and to do it; this I had to discover. I believed that God was trustworthy and that his ways are right and good no matter the conditions of life and now I wanted to know what he wanted of me. I had to learn a new way of thinking. I was no longer in control of my own life, he was. He alone would now influence the direction of my life; not me, my family, my nation or the world could do this any longer.

Don't copy the behavior and customs of

This world, but be a new and different person
With a fresh newness in all you do and think.
Then you will learn from your own experience
How his ways will really satisfy you.
Romans 12 (TLB)

I decided to start each day by asking God's will to be done in my life. I considered Romans 12 as basic to all prayers. Doing God's will was the only way I could experience freedom from all the struggles in my life. I had rebelled against God and now I wanted to live in his will and to do whatever he wanted me to do…but what did he want of me?

I read my Bible more and more, searching for answers. Where did he want me to be? What did he want me to do? As I read through the New Testament, I began to understand the difference between being a *believer* in Christ and being a *disciple* of Christ. I came to see that every disciple is a believer, but not every believer is a disciple! A believer is a person who comes to Christ in faith; this is the gift of God's grace. A disciple, however, becomes a servant of Jesus and is willing to pay the price for his faith. Believers inherit heaven, it is true, but disciples inherit a reward, as well. I was a changed man, different from whom I was; committed to becoming a disciple of Christ. The goals for my life were left behind; my ambitions were now set in a different direction. Each day, I experienced a new and more mature peace with God. I had fully yielded to the wisdom and goodness of his ways. I had been shown something of the nature of spiritual warfare, experiencing the realities of both the spiritual world and the Kingdom of God. Now God would change me even more as he opened another door in my life.

A missionary suggested I attend a 'Youth with a Mission' (YWAM) Discipleship Training School (DTS) on the island of Cyprus. I was hesitant to attend because it would mean leaving behind many precious things in my life: my home and family; my friends and relatives; everything that was familiar to me. If I were to take the training, it would also mean resigning my position in the army and loosing my salary. I wanted to learn more about the Bible, but I wasn't sure this was the right way. I wasn't even sure I was ready to do this! My parents were totally opposed to the plan. They asked some very pointed questions: How will you survive by yourself? Are you going to become destitute? Where will you get all the finances you need? All these questions added to my uncertainty.

I prayed, asking God to show me what he wanted. Again, through his Word, he gave me an answer:

'I tell you the truth,' Jesus replied, 'no one who has left home, or brothers or sisters or mother or father or children or fields for me and the gospel will fail to receive a hundred times as much in the present age (homes, parents, family, children, properties, fields…and with them persecution) and in the age to come eternal life.'

Mark 10:29-30 (NIV)

Even if I left all the people I loved and all the things for which I cared, I knew God would take care of me. Deep in my heart, I wanted to follow Jesus so I finally decided to go.

I made the decision while I was waiting to receive my first prosthesis. I couldn't wait to have the new l leg that would enable me to walk freely, without the help of people or crutches. I didn't get what I expected, though, and was greatly disappointed. I made several visits to a clinic in Haifa,

Israel, where they took measurements for the leg I would wear. Initially, I was full of hope, but then I experienced the pain caused by walking with it. I had not considered the practice it would take to learn again to walk. I was embarrassed at my clumsiness as I walked with it. I used the prosthesis, but as soon as I got home I would immediately take it off. It was a long time before I could adapt to it physically and emotionally. My physical handicap was very evident. I struggled in this learning process, but I continued to accept it as part of the course God had determined for me. In so many ways, my submission to God had brought me a peace and a joy that kept me moving forward. I wondered what the Lord would teach me next; what he wanted me to do. The lessons would continue on the island of Cyprus.

Chapter 8
The First Love

*It all sounds so glorious—transformation, change, conforming to
the image of Christ, but the servant is not above his master. Such
wondrous personal improvements come at the price of a personal cross*

Having made my decision to go to Cyprus, the time
had come for me to get a passport. Because this is not
easy for a Lebanese, arrangements were made to travel from
Israel. Also, I needed to raise money for the trip expenses,
the school fees, and for my personal needs. I wondered
where I would get the money since I couldn't work. My
missionary friend encouraged me to go on faith. "What do
you mean?" I asked. "Pray and ask God to provide for you,"
he replied. It was the first time in my life I had ever heard
something like this. I was used to working in order to earn
money and provide for my living. Just trusting the Lord to
provide by faith was an entirely new concept for me and it
ran right in the face of my culture and upbringing. To me it
was a shame to beg and the thought of possibly relying on
the Lord to provide through his people sounded very much
the same to me. I decided, though, to try and trust.

So much of this love walk with God was going to be a
new experience. Of course my parents were quite worried
about my decision, but my sisters encouraged me to take

this step of faith. I prayed with them and with some other believers and together we put the whole situation into the hands of the Lord. My sister Georgette gave me a gift of $250 for the trip. I still needed to come up with about $2000 more. I wanted to obey the Lord without hesitation and trusted he would provide the money in his way and in his timing.

The day to depart arrived. Everything was packed and I was ready. It was a very difficult goodbye for both my family and me. I was both excited about my new venture with God, but sad to be leaving all that was familiar. My missionary friend and I traveled by boat from Haifa, not Beirut. The trip took approximately 12 hours; an overnight journey and my first ever boat trip. I had to sit on a wooden chair on the deck the entire time. They gave each of us a mattress, but I couldn't fall asleep at all. I was sailing to an unknown new world, leaving behind everything from my past. As the ship crossed the Mediterranean Sea toward Cyprus, I was moving farther and farther from the world I loved. Despite being sad, even a little afraid, I knew that God was going to take care of me wherever I went. I knew God would help me overcome all the difficulties and hardships I might face. As we traveled, I turned in my Bible to Romans 8, once again, for comfort and encouragement, "Who shall separate us from the love of Christ? Shall trouble or hardship or persecution or famine or nakedness or danger or sword?"

The love of Christ is stronger than anything else in life. It was the only reason I left everything without regretting the losses. In the past, I did everything selfishly for myself. In a sense, I was the property of other people and even of Satan. I gained my freedom from both when I became the *possession* of Jesus Christ. No one can ever take this joy from me; the indescribable joy of giving my life over to Christ. I stood on the deck in the middle of the night, watching the moon reflecting on the water and feeling the mist of the sea's waves blowing refreshingly upon my face and was suddenly struck by the greatness of God's creation and the splendor of his majesty. It was God who was opening this new door for me! So He would have to help me walk through it and begin the work of learning the lessons he wanted to teach me. Perhaps, if I had realized how deeply entrenched I was in my culture and traditions, along with the current events of my country, I would have been more anxious about this trip than I already was. If I had known then how hard it would be to let all of it go and trust God to change me, I might have been completely overwhelmed. But in that moment, gazing out at the vastness of my God's creation, I trusted that he was able to do everything for me.

When we arrived at the port in Cyprus, people were waiting to meet us and to drive us to the school. It was evening when we arrived at the campus where nearly 100 students were gathered, anticipating our arrival. The room was filled with applause as soon as we entered. The speaker welcomed me and said, "We are happy to see you. Please introduce yourself." I stood in front of everyone feeling very embarrassed. My face turned red and I was scared as though I had never stood in front of people under such circumstances in my life. What could I say about myself? Everyone was staring at me. I wondered what they must have been thinking about me. Suddenly, I was overwhelmed by the thought that my physical appearance was unacceptable. It took me some time to form one coherent sentence. I was relieved when everyone started clapping again. Then the speaker said, "We were expecting you to arrive in a wheelchair, but we are very happy to see that you are able to walk!" I felt warmly welcomed and experienced a disarming kindness in this first meeting with my new classmates and the leadership of the school. The time spent in classes and life on the campus revealed my guarded personality and that it would need to be changed. To be transformed according to the pattern of Jesus would require a transparency and openness that the cultural customs of my Lebanese society had not encouraged. The prevailing atmosphere of acceptance during this time of training was my first experience with the love of God within the body of Christ. We truly were all brothers and sisters in a wonderful new family.

Physically exhausted from the long boat trip and emotionally challenged by the introduction at the school, I was eager to be shown to my room where I could privately begin the task of adjusting to my new circumstances. It was then that I discovered the close living quarters that the Holy Spirit would use as part of the breaking and humbling process of developing me into a disciple of Jesus. I was to be in one, small room with bunk beds and three other people! I was embarrassed for others to see the daily realities of living with a prosthesis and in this arrangement, I wouldn't be able to avoid it. When I later complained to my missionary friend, he simply smiled and said, "You will get used to it. Besides, you need to make new friends." I was challenged by the closeness and, at the same time, overwhelmed by a sense of isolation in such radically new surroundings. This was not going to be an easy experience. I would learn the openness among Jesus' disciples, as well as, the breadth of his love, receiving men and women from every nation. This was not going to be battlefield camaraderie. This would be something different.

The experiences of my life had taught me that anyone asking a lot of questions was suspicious and possibly dangerous, but here people gathered around in close quarters and, apparently in a friendly and truly interested manner, were asking me all kinds of questions about my life, my country, and my experiences. I could not bring myself to fully trust them and was suspicious, even somewhat afraid, especially of one roommate. He was from Egypt, clearly with a Muslim background, and had adopted the Christian name, Paul.

I sat in my first class session at the end of this long day of travel. It was the last lecture of the day for the others and it set the tone for what discipleship training was all about. The theme of the talk centered on the necessity and blessing of developing the habit of a personal, regular "quiet time" with the Lord. I was taught about spending time reading the Bible and hearing God's voice. My heart was touched to know that God wanted to spend time with me; he wanted me to be in his presence. It was referred to as 'being in fellowship' with God, meaning not only that he wanted me to speak to him but that God would speak to me. I wondered, would God really speak to me? Would I be able to hear his voice? When I went back to my room that night I wanted to practice what I had heard, but I was very tired and fell asleep right away. Over the next several weeks I continued to pray and read the Bible, always seeking to hear from God. As I waited in the silence, I wondered if some thing in my life was preventing me from hearing the Lord. Perhaps my pride or my complaining attitude was standing between me and my Lord. So I began to ask that God would change my heart attitudes and fill my life with love and humility.

One afternoon as I was sitting alone under a tree, considering the lesson of Samuel and Saul in I Samuel 15. I was crying during my prayer time; trying to open my heart to God, pouring out my concerns before him about many matters in my life. I was startled to hear a voice from heaven that said to me, "Elie, I love you." So real was the sound that I looked around, but no one was there. I knew it was the voice of God my Father. It made me tremble and my heart almost jumped out of my chest. The voice continued, "I will not leave you. I will bless your life. You are my son. I love you." The voice was very gentle, holy and pure. I stood up, looking for a place to hide. I felt like digging a hole in the ground and hiding there, but instead, I stood there crying. I could not understand why the Lord would love me. He again reassured me of his love and good intentions for my life. He felt so near to me. I could only praise him and thank him. There are no words to adequately express the personal sense of liberation I had in the confidence the love of God brought. Such great joy flowed from this confidence in God's love for me. It encouraged me to spend more time alone with him. The more time I spent reading the Bible and praying, the more he spoke to me. It was not always in the same way. At times it would be through the Scriptures, sometimes through leadership, and other times through dreams and visions. Always I was left with a sense of peace and comfort. God never left me feeling guilty or afraid.

Life in the Discipleship Training School was demanding and frustrating. Our daily schedule was rigorous and reminded me sometimes of life in the army, just friendlier! The days were carefully structured between classes and the expected exercise of spiritual disciplines, especially prayer and Bible study, allowing very little free time. As a grown man who had lived the libertine life of a soldier for years, some of the rules seemed unusually strict, even stifling. For example, the rules governing how to relate to the woman students seemed to be geared more to younger people; not someone as mature and experienced as I! I still was in the mindset of my old life and the habits I had formed. I came to understand these rules were part of the lessons for which God had brought me here.

Homesickness was an additional part of my struggles in adjusting to the new experiences at this school. As those first days went by, I was often lonely. I missed my family back home. I prayed for their safety and put them into the Lord's hands, especially as I heard about the political situation deteriorating in Lebanon. I was challenged by all of this, but I knew God had opened this door and trusted he had blessings in store if I would yield to the lessons meant to conform me into a disciple of the Lord Jesus.

The DTS experience was like a spiritual operating room where the Holy Spirit used the teachers and leaders to cut into our lives and begin the often painful work of removing the psychological scar tissue that remained from our old lives before coming to faith in Christ. Our teachers counseled us, opening up their own lives to us as they encouraged us get rid of...or as Scripture puts it, to 'reckon the old man dead in Christ'...the mindset of our former lives. They were advising us to discover and embrace all of the strength and the reality of our new life in Jesus. We were taught to see that old things had passed away and all things had become new. We were learning to change by coming to an ever-increasing awareness that by walking in the Spirit, we would be living out the new creation we had become in Christ.

One of the early steps I took in this process was the result of a growing conviction that God wanted me to be baptized. I wrestled over questions of whether or not it was necessary for me to be *re*baptized. I came to the conclusion that God was making no requirement of me to do so, but that it was my own desire and privilege to make a public declaration of my decision to be Jesus' disciple. I saw baptism as an act of obedience. It was not a saving act in and of itself. It didn't make me a Christian; that had happened when I believed that his death and resurrection dealt with my sins. My baptism was to be a testimony both to myself and to the world around me that I had been united with Jesus in his death and resurrection. I wanted to be a witness and to testify about God's work in my life. A date was set for my baptism. I was very excited. I was happy I had made this decision despite all the obstacles I thought were standing in the way. At the appointed time, I waded into the small pool with the leader, feeling a mixture of excitement and fear. My heart was racing. It was the first time that I would be able to testify so publicly about my faith in Jesus Christ. Everyone was crowded around us, watching as I proclaimed my faith and my commitment to obey my master. "Jesus Christ is my Lord and Savior. I will follow him till the last moment of my life. I will tell everyone about his salvation."

This testimony was given not only for the people around me. I did it also for myself. I was proclaiming out loud that I was a believer, I had a new identity in Christ, and from now on I would live as a true Christian. I knew it was a testimony to all the evil spirits that I was now the property of Jesus, King of Kings and Lord of Lords, and that I would follow Him no matter what. I declared I was willing to die for his sake and for the sake of spreading the Good News. This testimony broke the fear of Satan in my life. It gave me confidence that Satan was a conquered enemy because Jesus Christ was alive in me. God had redeemed me by his blood. It was good for me publicly to declare my identity in Jesus and proclaim that my future was secure because I belonged to him.

There were so many incidents that the Lord used to prick my conscience, forcing me to confront my pride, but it was a simple gesture on October 20 that would have a tremendous impact in helping me to break down the parochial ways I used to remain aloof and critical toward my fellow students. While all the students were having dinner in the large dining hall, the head of the school suddenly entered carrying a large cake in his arms. As he walked toward me everyone started singing, "Happy birthday, Elie." I was so embarrassed that I wanted to hide under the table. I was expected to blow out the candles and receive birthday greetings from everyone. Many gave me gifts and words of encouragement. It was the first time in my whole life anyone had ever celebrated my birthday. After the dinner and all of the festivities were over, I went to my room to consider what had happened. I got down on my knees and prayed for everyone who had been in the room. I thanked God for giving me such loving and wonderful brothers and sisters in the faith of Christ. I asked him to release me from my pride and replace it with love towards them. The change in my attitude was evident from that night on. I could see that the Holy Spirit was beginning a wonderful transformation of me, from the inside out. The classroom lectures became more and more alive to me; my ability to relate and develop friendships with my classmates developed quickly.

The tenderness of the fellowship between the students was an aspect of the school that caught me off guard. While I had longed for acceptance and real friendship all of my life, my nature and experiences of military life had made me remote and in ways, unapproachable. It was a challenge for me to embrace the unconditional love that came with being part of the body of Christ. I had difficulty building friendships because I did not know how to deal with the many cultural differences that were a part of the student body. Yet it seemed that the other students accepted me and were willing to accept my differences. It had always been very easy for me to criticize and find fault with people because this is how I had grown up. I was the first born, remember, and I was allowed to do this. Now I had to try to focus on the good qualities in people and appreciate them. Behind the judgment of others was a great deal of pride. It was time for me to give up my Middle Eastern lifestyle and stop being merely a Lebanese Christian. The Lord wanted me to become a catholic Christian in the true sense of belonging to the universal church of Jesus Christ as it exists in all the nations of the world. This challenge would shake me. The change would trouble me. Yet I knew the love of Christ would sustain me in making the transitions required to think with the same tender mercies that are a part of his nature and his commitment to all of humanity and all nations.

My identity was indeed changing from that self-centered firstborn son of Lebanon who had known only the ritual of a traditional structure of Christianity. The experiences of campus life and the classroom lessons of walking deeply with Jesus over the months were truly having their impact on me. We were taught a great deal about developing the inner work of the spiritual life. A great emphasis was place on the love of our heavenly Father. These lessons explained the vast difference between the perfections of a heavenly Father and the inevitable failures of our earthly fathers. Many times each of us were broken emotionally and there were many tears. We learned the importance not only of being forgiven, but of the necessity also to forgive. We came to understand that our presence at the Lord's Table required us to be reconciled not only with God, but also with our brothers and sisters on earth. The Middle Eastern mindset is very proud and puts a high priority on avoiding shame. It was very difficult to learn to say, "I'm sorry. I was wrong. Forgive me."

We learned too that the influence of demons in our lives could be the result of sins from the past and even curses that had been passed on from one generation to another. It was truly frightening to observe the practice of deliverance from these evil spiritual powers. It was also with great joy that we observed the liberty and healing that came when Jesus sets the captives free. We were learning of the great changes the Lord desires to make in our lives as we give ourselves to the practices of discipleship in order to serve him in very difficult world situations. We learned that there are two realms, the world and the kingdom of God. Day after day, we were presented with the option of living and walking in the Spirit. This walk would empower us to live out the kingdom of God in this world, living differently from which most of us had been living. Here we would experience the fruit of the Spirit in all tenderness and kindness. Love would be expressed toward all humanity, all nations, even our enemies. We were all learning about change, but I would also learn the powerful impact of putting those changes into real life experiences outside the classroom.

Chapter 9
The Power of Love

The classroom lessons of the Discipleship Training School changed more than just my thinking. It changed my heart to reflect God's universal compassion and interest...to love even our enemies.

Our daily lessons provided a solid foundation toward becoming disciples of Jesus. We were not just learning the Bible and the doctrines of the Christian faith, although we certainly did do that; we were being transformed by the power of the Holy Spirit according to the pattern shown us by Jesus. The lessons that most profoundly affected our lives happened outside the classroom as we lived and worked together; and shared our faith with the community around the school. These practical lessons were the ones that truly shaped us into disciples. We began to see our calling differently, understanding that it would often carry with it the painful suffering that often comes with being a Christ follower. God was changing all of us to view things from his perspective: his kingdom is a fellowship of those who name the name of Jesus from every tribe, tongue, and nation.

Our small school consisted of people from many different countries, backgrounds, and cultures. It was very difficult for me to have meaningful relationships with these people because deep inside, I believed all of my Lebanese traditions were superior and the experiences of my life were more significant than theirs. For their part, however, they seemed to be genuinely respectful and interested in my experiences and culture. Cross-cultural tolerance and appreciation have become standard courtesies now, but I was then a young Christian and had not yet considered that my homeland customs were not the only acceptable way of doing things.

Living together in such close conditions provided many opportunities to learn the customs of others. Lessons came to me in the simplest of situations, exposing my deep-seated root of pride and selfishness. Early one morning, I opened the refrigerator, looking for to something to eat, only to find different food items with name labels on them. One label read, "Please do not touch. This is the property of … " What? I had never seen such a thing in my life. I came to learn this is a common practice in many cultures, but in mine, you could open a refrigerator, even at a friend's house, and take whatever you wanted. It is part of Lebanese culture to give and to show generosity to family members and friends. If you were in a more formal setting, you knew never to take anything from someone the first time it was offered to you, but to wait until the offer was made two or three times. It is important to have some pride, even if you really wanted or needed what was being offered! The labeling of food in a refrigerator offended me. I understood it to be a selfish act. I started to boast to the other students about my culture, about the hospitality we offer, the beauty of my country, and about so many other practices that contributed to my sense of national pride. My prideful attitude made it difficult to build friendships. It seemed to me that no one understood me when I really just driving them away. I grew up very differently from the others I now found myself living with. I knew it was pride that made it impossible for me to accept people who were different. I wanted to be friendly with them, but I couldn't accept the differences.

Friendship was the best thing I ever experienced in my country and I wanted to find new friends in this phase of my life. To do that, I needed to change. As I prayed for change, the Lord began to teach me new lessons. I remembered God's words to me about love: I now had his love in my life and it was only through this love that I would be able to love others. I began to open up to those around me. I worked to stop putting on the "veil" when I was with people (the way my culture expressed hiding your true feelings). Although it was difficult, I began to reveal my inner feelings and thoughts. Many listened receptively and that made it easier for me to share my deepest pains and hurts. They encouraged me and prayed with me that God would deal with these matters. The classroom lessons were being worked out in real life. I even found myself able to say, "Please, forgive me." Never in my entire life had I ever apologized for anything I had done. Because those around me responded positively, I wanted to do the same for them. God's kingdom embraces every culture. He loves and calls people from all traditions. It was difficult for me to learn this lesson of God's love, but it made me see how vast the kingdom of God's reign is. I continued to be proud of my heritage, but no longer in an exclusive way. I was learning to value others and to hold humbly my own cultural experience…and to accept labels being placed on food!

Humility would become a continuous theme in my training. One of our lectures was about washing each other's feet. Jesus himself had set the example for us. The King of Kings knelt before his disciples and washed their dirty feet. Was it possible to be more humble than this? After washing their feet, Jesus said to his disciples, "…you should wash one another's feet. I have set an example and you should do as I have done for you…Now that you know these things you will be blessed if you do them." (John 13:14-17) I wanted to participate in such a ceremony. I wanted to do the difficult thing, to humble myself before believers who were different than I, but also chosen by my Lord. One night, we held such a ceremony at school.

I found myself holding a jar of water. I put a towel around my waist. Then I looked around the room, seeking to find someone that I did not like. I saw a man from a nation that is an enemy to my own and I determined to wash his feet. This was an opportunity to break my pride and the resentment that I had towards this man and his nation. In this world, his home country was an enemy to mine, but in the kingdom of God, we were spiritual brothers. I did not want to continue hating this person; I wanted to love him just as Jesus loved him. I stood before him and then knelt down to begin. As I started washing his feet, the presence of the Lord filled the place. I blessed this man and asked for his forgiveness. He fell upon my shoulder and started to cry. "Please don't wash my feet," he wept. "I am the one who should be asking forgiveness from you. Please forgive me and my country." It was a sacred moment. I washed his feet with joy. This experience changed my life and filled me with such joy I knew that I could do it again without hesitation.

Lessons in humility also came in surprising ways. On one wall of the training school was a big board where notes and information were posted to let us know of coming events. One morning, I stopped by to read what was on the board. One notice caught my eye. I was surprised to find my name, Elie Hasbani, included on a list of names of people who owed the school money. Beside my name was the message, "$1200 debt for school expenses; please pray or help." I had forgotten about this debt! I was embarrassed that it had been publicly posted for all to see. Where could I get this money? I couldn't call my parents and ask them to send money because they were against my coming to this school. I had no solution for paying this debt. I even considered leaving the school and return to my country. I ran to my room. There, I decided to fast and pray for three days. I was slowly learning that God could provide for my needs if he chose to. I knew it would only be the Lord's provision that could solve this.

On the last day of my fast I was sitting on my bed praying when I heard a knock on the door. A woman came in with an envelope in her hand. She handed it to me and said, "I was praying and the Lord told me to give you this." Then she left the room without giving me a chance to ask for an explanation. I opened the envelope and, to my surprise, there was a large amount of money in it. I counted it, over and over again. I could not believe what she had given me! It was $1500, $300 more than I needed. I jumped up and down on my bed until I hit my head on the upper bunk! I was delirious with excitement, in pain, but oh so happy! I sat down again and thanked the Lord for answering my prayer. He had even given me more than I had asked for. I went straight to the school office and paid off my debt. I still had $300 and I felt the Lord leading me to give this amount to another brother who also had a debt to pay for schooling. When I gave him the gift, my joy was doubled. I experienced the joy of giving and the joy of receiving. I never knew that it would feel so good to receive something as a gift from the Lord.

Perhaps no lesson was greater than learning to forgive. God the Father is our example, forgiving all of the wrong committed against him through Jesus Christ. As his disciple, I was learning that I could do no less. Jesus lived an example of the unconditional love of our heavenly Father when he forgave those who hated him. While hanging on the cross, he asked the Father to forgive those who had nailed his body to the wooden structure, understanding they didn't know what they were doing. I harbored a great deal of hatred and bitterness within. I held tightly to the events in my life. Even though it looked like I had moved passed them, I really had allowed my pain to grow deep within me. At the school, I was learning that the Father makes one family of all sinners, not just those who share the same cultural experiences. If I was going to be his servant, a world Christian, I needed to make his mindset mine. I had to have a deep love for the people who were from countries other than Lebanon, including a love for my enemies who hated me, and even for those of other religions, including Islam.

As the school year progressed and the teaching phase had been completed, we entered a practical phase. Five groups were created and each was assigned to a different country for training. We could choose between five countries—Jordan, Egypt, Lebanon, Iraq, or Turkey. I chose to go with the group heading to Egypt, but when I applied for a visa, I was turned down. I wondered why God closed that door for me. I was really looking forward to going. All of the other teams left and I had to stay in Cyprus. I decided to join the team that was already established in Cyprus, but worked in a different area than the location of the school in Limassol. Every day we went out into the streets to meet with people and tell them about Jesus Christ. On Fridays, we would pray the whole day and then, late in the afternoon, go out and do a street event. We would start by worshiping through music and as people gathered around us, some of the members of the team would perform a sketch about sin and its terrible consequences; the rest of the team would pray for the people, asking God to open their hearts to accept his Word.

One day, during the little drama, I asked God to lead me to someone to talk to about the salvation Jesus offers. I was drawn to a man who looked like an Arab. As I began to walk toward him, I became scared. Three times this happened. Shaking, I opened my Bible to read something that might give me direction. I came to these words, "Do not be afraid; have courage, for I am with you," and "Open your mouth and I will fill it with words." I moved forward and stood by the man and asked him, "Good play, isn't it?"

"Yes," he said, "But I didn't understand anything. They are talking about Christ, aren't they? They are trying to fool all these people." I didn't know what to reply, so I asked him where he was from, even though I already knew from his accent that he was from Lebanon. "I'm from Lebanon," he answered. "Where in Lebanon?" "From the south of Lebanon. From Tyre," he answered. "I am from the south too," "What is your name?" "Mohammed," he replied. Suddenly my tongue got tangled in my mouth and I couldn't speak. This man was a Muslim. Millions of thoughts ran through my mind before I was able to speak again. I still had bitterness in my heart toward Muslims! Many of them were our enemies during the war. Is salvation for them as well? I was not ready to give him the message of peace and tell him about salvation. I forgot I was standing before someone who had the same need for salvation as I once had. The only thing I could think about was my hatred of him. I did not care if he got saved or not!

Mohammed broke my chain of thoughts when he asked, "What part of the south are you from?" "Deir Mimas," I responded. And then he knew that I was a Christian. He asked me if I was with this group and I answered that I was. He continued to ask me why we were doing this? Why were we evangelizing on the street? What did we want to tell these people? I felt attacked and was speechless, but then I realized he was coming right out and asking me to tell him about the Good News in Jesus Christ! I shared my testimony with him and how the Lord saved and changed me. I did not want to get into a theological discussion about doctrines I knew would be controversial for a Muslim. I continued to pray in my heart as I was sharing with him. He was fully attentive and interested. I did not know what was going on inside of him until I noticed that he was crying. Then he said to me, "I need this Christ you are talking about." I told him he could ask Jesus to come into his life right then, right there. I explained that Jesus was there with us and was willing to save him from his sins, just as he had done for me. I heard Mohammed say, "Jesus, I believe in you as the Son of God. Please come into my life and save me!"

I could not believe what was happening. The first person I shared with, the first one to give his life to Christ, was an *enemy* of mine. From that moment on Mohammed and I shared the same goal, the same future, and the same salvation. His conversion was a turning point in my life regarding my relationship with Muslims. God was showing me his great love for all humanity and how I could do the same. My heart was changing. God had answered my prayers; I had a new inner strength to forgive.

After this, Mohammed and I developed a friendship. We met regularly, prayed together, read the Bible, and even worshiped together. The walls that I had built between my enemies and myself had been broken down. I was given the chance to confess to him my hatred and that I was wrong. I asked him to forgive me for all the hatred and bitterness I harbored. My willingness to forgive replaced my hatred with God's love. This was not an easy step. It takes a work of grace and the power of the Holy Spirit in one's life to heal the wounds of the past and turn from hatred to forgiveness and loving your enemies. Jesus had given me a powerful experience so I could understand what he meant when he said, "You have heard that it was said: Love your neighbor and hate your enemy. But I tell you, love your enemies and pray for those who persecute you, that you may be sons of your Father in heaven." (Matthew 5:43-45a)

So much of my youth, all of my experiences in civil war, the daily reality of walking with only one real leg—these all told me that I should hate Muslims. Now I was being taught by God that while Islam may be a false religion that can lead to so much error and violence, Muslims are people that he loves and longs to save just as he had done for me. I understood that God wanted me to have compassion for Muslims who are often in a deep, spiritual battle; to feel for them as God himself does. I began to understand the impact evil had to imprison the lives and hearts of Muslim people. I came to understand the biblical teaching that the battle is not against flesh and blood, but against spiritual wickedness in high places. He wanted me to clearly see and understand the great power of the gospel, through the Holy Spirit, to save.

It was our custom at the DTS in Limassol to have an outreach supper every Friday night. The format of these evenings was a simple supper followed by a time of fellowship and sharing. One evening, one of our Swiss students invited a man named Ali, a Lebanese Muslim living at the time on Cyprus. The guest speaker that evening wanted to pray personally for individuals. As he prayed for an Egyptian man, the Holy Spirit fell on him with glorious manifestations such that Ali and the other guest Muslims were awe-struck when they witnessed this genuine outpouring of power and redemption on the life of a humble man seeking God. This beautiful demonstration of the Holy Spirit resulted in mixed reactions Ali left in anger; other Palestinian Muslims went out to get their friends to come and see "the real Christians." God was at work; Satan was angry; and spiritual warfare was being fully engaged.

Ali called me the next day and asked if I would come and talk with him. As we discussed the events of the previous evening over tea, Ali was especially angry that the speaker who had prayed with such obvious effect had claimed that God spoke to him. I explained that Christians first hear from God by reading the Scriptures, but that they can also at times hear from the Lord through the power of the Holy Spirit. I asked him, "Can Mohammed speak to you?" He said yes. He then turned toward Mecca and he began to pray. At that moment, God spoke to my heart… Elie, I want you to watch. I will teach you an important lesson. As Ali prayed and I watched, an evil spirit descended upon him and possessed him. I was at first afraid because Ali was clearly overcome with fear and troubled. He was sweating profusely and unable even to speak. As he suffered under the frightening power and influence of the enemy, God gave me a great peace, an understanding to see the difference between the manipulation of demons manifest in Ali and the grace-filled blessing of the coming-along-side-of comfort of the Holy Spirit we had witnessed the evening before. As Ali came out of his trance, I was able to share this lesson with him. Even though Ali had so clearly seen the gentle and good distinction between the Holy Spirit of Christianity and the jinn of Islam, he was spiritually bound and made his choice to be separated from the truth. I could see so clearly the difference between two spiritual realms: one of saving grace and the other of angry bondage. God was teaching me that my enemies were actually those of the spiritual realm. My human 'enemies' were in truth captivated by those spirits and place in miserable bondage. I could no longer hate them. I now had tremendous compassion for their predicament: slavery to the devil and his evil angels.

This was one of the more disappointing experiences because Ali walked away from knowing the one true God. Happier contacts resulted in individuals deciding for Jesus' kingdom. We had an outreach event in one of the mosques of Limassol. We had worked to be on friendly terms with the leaders of this mosque. The local muezzin (the crier who announces the Muslim hours of prayer) invited my friend Robin and myself to hear a traveling sheik who was going to be speaking at the mosque. Of course Mazen, the muezzin, was hoping to win us as converts to Islam. He did not know that God was seeking to win him to Jesus Christ. We accepted his invitation and came to hear the sheik speak. After the normal prayers were completed, the sheik got up to preach on how to please Allah. The core of his message was that giving to the building of mosques was the road to pleasing Allah and winning his favor for paradise. Once again I had the experience of seeing an evil spirit descend upon the sheik as he spoke. I wondered if the spirit was intimidated by the presence of Christians because it was so obvious the sheik would look to both his left and his right, but he would never look straight ahead at us. When the sheik finished speaking, the people emptied their pockets and filled a large tray with their money to build mosques. God was not finished with Mazen, though. As is the custom, we responded to his friendship and invitation by asking him to visit our church service…and he accepted! His experience among us left him surprised. He had not witnessed before the joyfulness experienced in Christian worship. As he visited again and again, he began to join in the celebration of happy praise and soon lifted his hands in submission to the Lordship of Jesus Christ. His journey would not be easy as his conversion to Christianity brought the inevitable rejection and persecution from Muslim friends and family. He found peace for his life in life of Jesus. We learned in a new and fresh way that the power of the gospel is to be found when the church is alive with the Holy Spirit and his power.

These lessons could not have been learned in the classroom alone. They are gained through life experiences in the power of Christ; valuable lessons in Christian maturity. As the end of the school year approached in 1988, I anticipated my return to Lebanon with several urgent matters of prayer. I had questions about the nature of my calling and ministry in the future. My vision of the church had expanded to the nations. I was now seeing the love and calling of God to every tongue and tribe. I was ready to jump out into the entire world. For now, God seemed to be calling me back to Lebanon…but why?

PART IV
BATTLE FIELD CHANGED

Chapter 10
New Spiritual Battle

I left Lebanon after military training and service—death had frightened me because it seemed to have no purpose. Now I was returning to Lebanon after training in a spiritual army and I could face even death, unafraid, because of the new purpose for which I lived.

I had completed two sessions of Discipleship Training School at the Youth With A Mission's facility in the remote interior of Cyprus and one session of their School of Missions near the port town of Limassol. As the school year was coming to a close, it became clear the Lord wanted me to return to Lebanon. A guest evangelist at the school related miracles of God experienced by those bringing Bibles into various countries around the world, specifically Arab nations. After he finished his series of lectures, we all started praying for these Arab countries and the whole of the Middle East. When we began to pray for Lebanon, I felt chills all over. I prayed with all my heart and shouted out to the Lord for his mercy to fall on my homeland. God was reviving my love for my country. As I prayed, I told the Lord that I was willing to return to Lebanon and if necessary die for Him there, for the sake of the good news of His kingdom. "Reveal yourself to them," I prayed fervently. "Save them as you saved me." The other students and leaders gathered around me and joined in tearful prayers for the repentance and forgiveness of the people of Lebanon.

The biblical lesson of Queen Esther informed the first step in returning to my country. Just as she had interceded with God for the sake of her people, I fasted and prayed for three days for the sake of mine. As I waited on the Lord, He made it clear to me in dreams and visions, along with the encouragement of his people that my first step in becoming a light to the nations of the earth was to return initially to my own nation, Lebanon. And so I prepared to return home. I again stepped onto a boat that would take me back to my homeland, but not before being in prayer with the Christians I had spent so much time with during my training. I was so excited at the idea of seeing my family, my friends, and my country again. I was returning as a very different person than I was when I had left them. I had a new heart and new weapons—the weapons of peace, love, and reconciliation. I was returning home with a new attitude, a desire to share the Christian message of love with all of the Lebanese people, no matter what group or party or religious background to which they belonged. I was a changed man in many ways. What I did not anticipate was how little had changed in Lebanon. I did not foresee the clash that my new perspective would make with the conflicting parties who did not understand the love and reconciliation of God as I had come to know it.

The boat took me to Beirut where I was to stay for several weeks before going back to my village in the south of the country. In Beirut, I stayed with some of my relatives who questioned me about my time in Cyprus. I shared with them what Christ was teaching me and what he was doing in my life. I was surprised by the way they responded to my words. They made fun of me and ridiculed not only me, but my faith as well. "How much did they pay you to follow them? How much will you pay us if we follow? Do you worship saints?" They became very angry with me when I told them that I did not worship saints. Near their house was a large statue of Saint Elijah (my namesake) to whom they prayed daily. They said, "You carry the name of this saint! So why don't you worship him?" I explained that it was just a piece of stone someone had sculpted; it cannot hear you; I pray to the living God who can hear and answer my prayers. They didn't understand. This reception was very difficult for me. It was only my first week back in Lebanon and already I was facing rejection. I prayed that God would reveal to them that He is the only one who can save, protect, and answer prayers. Two days later the area was severely bombed and one of the bombs hit the statue and completely destroyed it. The people were so disturbed by this incident that they said to me, "Did you come here to have us killed?" I asked them how a statue that could not even protect itself would ever be able to protect them.

As I prayed for these people, I couldn't help but remember again Lebanon's historical roots in idolatry. We were the descendants of the ancient Phoenicians who worshiped Baal, practicing all of the evil elements of that idolatry. This Baal worship impacted the ancient Israelites when King Ahab made a treaty with the king of Tyre and married his daughter, Jezebel. Oh, how the prophet Elijah railed against this and the worship of Baal that came with the marriage. Is it possible, I reasoned, that the spirit of Baal is still somehow in the heart of the Lebanese people? Is this why I was facing such ridicule for my faith? Although the Catholic Church had never taught or intended believers to worship saints or pray to statues, had the ancient root of idolatry turned the pious practices of Christianity into false worship? My prayers for family and friends focused more on deliverance from spiritual bondage from that point on. Salvation would require not merely the intellectual arguments of men, but also the power and victory of the Holy Spirit over these long seated spiritual forces. I had suffered a type of bondage to a cultural Christianity of state ID cards. God had rescued me from this situation and I trust that he was willing and able to win them as well.

After spending some time visiting different churches that taught the Bible and a personal faith in Jesus (I was longing to find a church home), I turned south and headed toward Deir Mimas, toward home, family, and friends. I was warmly welcomed. I felt accepted and wanted. I stayed for about six months, going from village to village, both Muslim and Christian, telling everyone what the Lord had done for me. I went up into the mountains for a season of prayer. I cried out for the Lord to save these people, both Christian and Muslim. My desire was that the now closed road between Israel and Lebanon would once again become an open highway for the spread of the gospel. Just as in the early times of Jesus' disciples, when the new believers spread northward from Jerusalem and the road became a gospel highway to Damascus and Antioch, so I prayed that such a spread of the gospel would happen again. I was confident God was using me among these people. The first people to pray and accept Jesus were my two brothers and a sister. I also knew that my brother-in-law, one of my best friends, had given his life to the Lord. This gave me great joy.

It wasn't all joyous, however. Some accused me of being a Jehovah's Witness while others said I was a member of a cult who had been brainwashed. Because I did not worship the saints, they said I was not a Christian and that I had received satanic teaching. Some even accused me of being a spy for some of the political factions. I was called a liar because they knew my past and could not believe I had changed. Some tried to draw me back into the life I used to live; others tried to hit me to see if I would strike back. They couldn't understand why I was calling for reconciliation and love. A group of believers who prayed with me brought some comfort, but as the rejection continued to increased, I was reminded of the words of Jesus, "A prophet is honored everywhere except in his hometown and among his relatives and his own family."

I knew I needed to be part of a community of faith in a congregational setting so began looking for the right place. I felt my heart being drawn to the Church of God in Beirut, but as so often happens when we are seeking to follow the leadings of God, I was not sure I was right. But God was willing and able to confirm for me the certainty of his leading. As I continued to wait on him for direction, my sister Georgette came to me one day and said that an old woman in another village had given her a message for me. God had spoken to her in a dream with the directive to assure Elie that he was supposed to go to the Church of God in Beirut where the Lord would work out the details for him. How thankful I was that God would confirm in this manner the path I was to follow. I was reminded of the words in Psalm 32, "I will instruct you and teach you in the way you should go; I will counsel you and watch over you. Do not be like the horse or the mule, which have no understanding, but must be controlled by bit and bridle or they will not come to you." (NIV) Was I acting like a dumb mule in not immediately following the leadings of God?! Perhaps, but I was also learning I could count on God to confirm his will for my life when I am unsure.

With this confirmation, I moved to Beirut. I asked the taxi driver I had hired to take me straight to the Church of God. He did not know where it was, so I told him just to drive me to the area and I would find it. He stopped on a busy street full of shops. I got out of the car and went into a fabric store to ask for directions. As soon as I asked the clerk about the church a big smile appeared on his face, "I am an elder of this church!" He picked up the phone and immediately called the pastor and told him to expect us. The pastor welcomed me warmly and, while having tea together, I shared my testimony with him. I had no idea what to do next or where to stay, but God had promised me He would show me the way step by step. The pastor said, "I have been praying for someone to help me and stay with me. There is a room on the upper floor where you can live. Every morning we will be able to pray together." I loved my time there.

I was given a small salary and began my ministry according to the pastor's bidding. My first duties were not an important spiritual responsibility, but rather the simple tasks of a servant. Much of what I did was considered 'woman's work' while I was growing up. I was expected to clean the church and to prepare it for meetings. I was asked to clean windows, dust the chairs, distribute hymnbooks, and so on. I cannot deny that I was shocked at first, especially since I had never done such chores in my life. I was not convinced this was the kind of work I should be doing, but I agreed to do it because the Lord had brought me to this place.

An old man who was a member of the church became very sick and had no one to take care of him. They sent me to stay with him for a week to help him. That time seemed like a year to me. He was unable to communicate with me because he was so weak. I fed him, helped him go to the bathroom, changed his clothes, and bathed him. These were things I had never done for anyone. We slept in the same room and one night, I was awakened by a noise. I jumped up and approached the old man. I found him sitting up in his bed, talking as if someone were there having a conversation with him. I looked around to see if there was someone in the room other than the two of us. I was scared and couldn't sleep so I sat with him, watching him constantly. He stayed awake for several hours doing all kinds of strange things. He held both of his hands up and acted as if he were trying to put thread into the hole of a needle. His hands were empty, but he kept trying for almost an hour until he believed that he had accomplished his mission. He was tired and went back to sleep, but I was unable to do so. I prayed the rest of the night and into the next morning. I don't remember how I survived the week, but I knew one thing: God cared for this man. He had been a faithful servant his whole life; now I was serving God by being a servant and meeting the needs of an old saint.

The church was in need of a worship leader so that became part of my work, too. This was a difficult task for since I had no musical training and was not able to read musical notation very well. I had to choose songs according to the theme of the service and coordinate everything with the church pianist. I had to practice songs over and over until I got them. Sometimes members of the congregation would choose songs and since I had not rehearsed them, I couldn't lead! I remember once when someone picked a song and told us the number, everyone opened their hymnbooks and started to sing. Everyone except me! I forgot what number it was and kept searching for the song until the entire hymn was over. I was so embarrassed and wanted to stop being the worship leader. Sometimes members of the church would come to me after the service and comment on my leadership or singing or even my hand gestures. Many times my feelings were hurt, but the pastor encouraged me to continue. Serving in this position offered few honors or rewards, but I learned to be faithful even in sometimes embarrassing situations.

The pastor and I continued to pray together each day. After one of those times, he explained to me that if I wanted to continue serving the church, it would be good for me to attend a Bible College and earn a degree. This would provide me with a better knowledge of the Word of God and be more accepted by the church. This was not an easy decision to make. How could I go back to school and study? It had been years since I had been in any formal school situation. Where would I get the money for necessary expenses? I knew the pastor's advice was right so I was determined to find a way, asking God to provide again for what I saw as impossible.

A week later I registered at the Mediterranean Bible College in Beirut. It was a small college with strict rules and a very disciplined atmosphere, unlike any other school I had ever attended. The thirty students with whom I was studying had higher degrees than I and were very hard working. It took me several months to get accustomed to the school. I had adapted to the school in Cyprus and to the pastors home, but now I had to follow new rules, obeying the bell from Tuesday to Friday, 8:00 AM to 6:00 PM. We were required to study for six hours a day and spend at least one hour in prayer. Being alone with women was strictly forbidden. The only time we could converse was for a few stolen moments before or after class or while finishing our regular duties such as washing dishes. It was one of the philosophies of the school to teach discipline and obedience. Even though it was a difficult time for me, it was just the kind of training I needed. My sister, Diana, enrolled at the same Bible college. It was so good to have her around; she was a great support and encouragement for me.

This was a very busy time in my life. In addition to the MBC courses, I completed six months of training with Campus Crusade for Christ. My pastor kept me involved in visiting other churches, schools, and the church members in their homes./ Once an evangelical school invited us to share during their daily chapel time. I received invitations to share my testimony, one at a school where I was able to speak to over 500 students and faculty. The Lord touched many of them and I had the opportunity to answer their questions and counsel them on spiritual matters. During that same time, our pastor took a six-week sabbatical leaving me with additional responsibilities with the church.

Busy or not, I couldn't ignore that the political situation was again becoming worse. Early in the Lebanese civil war the government had invited Syria to enter the country with military forces, hoping they would be able to deal with the violence being perpetrated against Christians by the radical

Muslim PLO. When Egypt, and eventually Jordan, made peace with Israel in the late 1970's, Syria's allegiance shifted. Syria became another dangerous enemy to the Christian population of Lebanon. In 1989, as I was beginning ministry work in Beirut, the Christian militia under General Aoun declared a war of liberation against the Syrians and their mostly Muslim allies. This vicious conflict, just as the civil war itself was drawing to a close, accomplished nothing militarily. It resulted mostly in the destruction of much of Christian east Beirut. It became necessary for us to fight for survival and we daily faced the possibility of death. God provided many opportunities at this time to minister to the spiritual and physical needs of hurting people.

The college had a bomb shelter under its building. During this conflict, neighbors from the surrounding area came and spent many days and nights with us in the shelter. They felt safe there. Because of the circumstances in the city, they were open to us praying with them. We held daily meetings where we sang, prayed, and read the Bible. Many people who never had attended any church before gave their lives to the Lord during those days.

It was a very tense time in the city. The shelter caught on fire one evening, but we were able to keep it under control. Stores and houses burned down either from the bombing or from unattended candles used in the dark night hours when there was no electricity. The college was open only if the situation allowed and many times classes were canceled because there was little or no attendance. To make matters even worse, the fuel tanks that supplied all of Beirut exploded. The skies were dark for two days. This affected most of the trees and grass, even the cedars of Lebanon

As I saw the destruction around me, again and again I was reminded whom our fight was against. The physical destruction was the result of the battle against spiritual wickedness in high places. I continually prayed that God would have mercy on my country. We formed groups of young men from the church to go out weekly and share the message of Jesus Christ. Many young people gave their lives to Christ and found freedom from their addiction to drugs and alcohol. With believers from congregations other than our own, we began to discover our joint responsibility as members of the Body of Christ; to work together to share the good news, trusting Jesus Christ as Savior and Lord. The head pastor of the Church of God under whom I was working, was also the head of the Lebanese Bible Society. This gave me many opportunities to work with pastors of other churches. There were even opportunities to speak with Orthodox and Catholic priests and churches. Working together brought a new joy in ministry. We gathered weekly to pray for our city. The Holy Spirit was present in our meetings and we experienced a unity among us. This unity resulted in spiritual growth, miracles of healing, and many, including Muslims, coming to faith in Christ. Church members were emboldened by God to share the gospel even in very dangerous situations. We experienced Jesus as the Prince of Peace, one of his titles from the Bible. He alone would be able to overcome the tragedy of the war that surrounded us. No peace process, whether from the United Nations or the United States, would be able to deliver from this war. I was convinced by working along side of believers from different backgrounds that part of my service to God would be as a man of peace and not a man of war.

Having now walked with the Lord Jesus for several years, I was beginning to appreciate the idea that our Christian life is a pilgrimage. We are in this for the long haul and it is a process of maturing. Once we have submitted to his lordship, our lives become a work of change and progress toward becoming mature disciples. I was beginning to see that it takes time for old habits to be broken and for new Christ-like habits to form. I considered Moses who spent 40 years in the Midian dessert; Paul who waited on God for years in the Arabian Desert; and others like David, all of whom discovered that the walk of becoming a disciple of the living God is a journey of change. I desired another change to my life. If it was the Lord's will, I hoped to find a wife to be part of the journey; who would share with me the calling and ministry to the community of God. How God chose to fulfill that hope is a story in itself!

Chapter 11
Bride From Lebanon

God said, "It isn't good for man to be alone; I will make a companion for him, a helper suitable for him"...so the Lord God

Elie and Luna

I prayed daily for the opportunity to meet the woman who would share the rest of my life. I prayed specifically for a believer who would understand and love me. I needed a woman who would accept me just as I was and who would be my partner; one who would complement my weaknesses. I was always looking around me, in different churches and ministries, for the right one, but how would I know she was the right one? I met several women, but nothing worked out. The Lord either said "No" or I felt something was missing. I made a conscious decision to spend more time studying and serving others, just to forget the loneliness I felt. I determined to trust that if the desire in my heart was from God and according to his will, he would be in the details and responsible to choose my bride. Our paths would cross when the time was right.

I felt that my prayer was like that of the Hebrew poet in the fourth chapter of the Song of Solomon: "Come with me from Lebanon, my bride. We will look down from the summit of the mountain, from the top of Mount Hermon, where the lions have their dens, and panther prowl. You have ravished my heart, my lovely one, my bride; I am overcome by one glance of your eyes, by a single bead of your necklace. How sweet is your love, my darling, my bride. How much better it is than mere wine. The perfume of your love is more fragrant than all the richest   spices. Your lips, my dear, are made of honey. Yes, honey and cream are under your tongue, and the scent of your garments is like the scent of the mountains and cedars of Lebanon." The difference, however, between the Hebrew poet and myself was that he knew who his loved one was. I did not!

I developed some great friendships while at the Bible college. I was part of a circle of friends that went out on a regular basis just to have fun together. My sister was also part of this group. One of the guys, Costy, became my best friend and his sister, Luna, was my sister's. We spent most of our free time together and this group became very close friends. Before I realized it, I found myself paying more attention to Luna. She was also a student at Mediterranean Bible College and worked as the college librarian. I could not stop my feet from going to the library! Once I got there, I would not leave unless something extremely urgent called me away. I couldn't believe how quickly my love for books had grown! Many times I pretended I was studying when in reality I was watching her do her work. I could not take my eyes off her beautiful face and flowing hair. Fortunately, no one noticed my stargazing, not even her. The only way I could speak to her was to ask for help in finding a book I couldn't find on my own or didn't want to! So my literary interests increased greatly!

Even though we were good friends within the group, it was very hard for me to speak to her privately. I had never felt this way toward anyone else in my life. I could not understand what was going on with me! I knew the time she arrived at the college in the morning. I would wait downstairs by the elevators, pretending I had just arrived, and then remark how it was such a coincidence that we had run into each other. This is what I had to do in order to have a little time to speak to her alone. To see her smile was enough to make my day. Many of the courses we were taking were given in English so I often came to her for help, to explain to me some English words or even pages that I did not understand. I learned a great deal about her through these brief encounters. She was the daughter of a pastor. She had given her life to Jesus when she was five years old. She grew up in the church community. Her parents had been responsible for a girls orphanage for more than fifteen years.

She studied journalism in college for two years before she decided to quit and focus on theology at MBC.

I started to pray more seriously about Luna. I wanted to know what God had to say about this matter and not make decisions based on my emotions. Deep inside of me, something seemed to be directing all of my heart and thinking...and fixing it on her. As the months flew by, I realized that I was falling in love with Luna. I was frustrated because I could not express my love to her. I spent three days in prayer and fasting in order to know God's will for Luna and myself. The Lord began to speak to me from his Word. One verse kept coming before me: "Joseph, son of David, do not be afraid to take Mary home as your wife." The Lord convinced me to replace the names with our own as I read the verses: "Elie, do not be afraid to take Luna home as your wife." This verse encouraged me a great deal. It was a kind of confirmation for me from the Lord that my choice was his choice. My love for her increased as I prayed for her. She became part of my life. She began to notice the advances that I was making and she never turned me away. We continued going out with the group of friends; many times I found myself alone with her and yet unable to speak. I really did not know how to talk to one as pure and sweet as Luna.

With the start of Christmas vacation that year, my sister went home to Deir Mimas to be with the rest of the family, but I decided to spend Christmas in Beirut. I regularly visited the orphanage where Luna's father worked. Knowing I had not gone home, Luna's father invited me to spend Christmas Eve with his family; he invited me to come to their apartment where Luna and her family would be celebrating the holiday. Of course, I accepted! That evening, after dinner, we spent some time singing Christmas carols. Between each song Luna's father would read a passage from Scripture. The first verse he read that night was, "Joseph, son of David, do not be afraid to take Mary home as your wife." He stopped reading there and closed the Bible. Something welled up inside of me and I shouted, "Amen!" Everyone turned to look at me with bewildered looks on their faces. I went home that evening, happy and assured the Lord really wanted Luna for me. Now I was confident to look for the next opportunity to talk to her about my feelings and to open my heart to her.

The next day, Christmas morning, the phone rang at the church office where I was praying alone. I was surprised to hear Luna's voice inviting me for lunch that day. I hurried to their house, certain that this was the perfect opportunity for me to talk to her. After eating, Luna went to the kitchen to prepare coffee and I found myself alone in the living room. I wandered to the balcony where Luna found me when she returned with the coffee. There were some awkward moments as we stood sipping our coffee. Finally, with a trembling voice, I said, "Luna, I have something to tell you."

"What is it?" she asked calmly.

"What I am about to tell you is very important for both of us!"

"OK," she said nonchalantly. "Go ahead."

I cleared my throat. "Frankly, I've been thinking about you all the time. And I've been praying too!"

She stared at me. "What are you trying to say, Elie?"

"Luna, I love you. I'm sure of my feelings. I am not just fooling around. I'm serious and I am thinking of marriage!"

She tried to keep her laughter inside herself but failed. I wasn't sure what she thought was so funny and her casual attitude did not help me a bit. Yet I decided to get everything off my chest. "I prayed about us and the Lord gave me an answer. That's why I'm asking you. I want you to pray before giving me your answer. And I want you to take into consideration my leg situation. Get a confirmation from the Lord. When you have an answer, please let me know."

Nothing came out of her mouth. Then she started laughing again. I could not understand why she was laughing or what she was thinking. She turned and went inside while I stood on the balcony paralyzed. I stood there for half an hour confused and uncertain. I spent the whole afternoon at their home feeling dazed. Finally, I went home. Unable to sleep that night, I prayed for Luna, asking the Lord to reveal his will to her clearly…and soon! A week later she came to see me. Without any hesitation, she came to me and said, "I think my answer is yes."

"You think?" I said incredulously. "I want you to be certain. Go back home and pray some more and be sure!" I wanted to accept her "Yes," but at the same time I did not want there to be any hesitation on her part.

At that same time the fighting in Lebanon once again became very severe. It was different this time because it was Christian against Christian. The government in Beirut was seeking to resolve the civil war and it took a stand against the Christian militias and army. The Christian regions were even divided against each other and bombing started from both sides. There were so many different factions and political parties of both Muslims and Christians that it was difficult to know who would be the next deadly enemy.

People were trapped in their homes or in shelters for days. It was dangerous to walk around on the streets because there were snipers shooting to kill anyone who came into view. No distinction was made between military personnel and civilians. Lives were lost; fear and anxiety overcame the people. There was a shortage of food and an absence of civil services. I was so glad I was no longer actively involved in the war as before. God had now put me in a position to help other people. Bombing became intense. The country was divided by blocked and mined roads, disconnected phone lines, and a failure of electrical service. For nine days, Luna and I were not able to communicate. I was very worried, but there was no way to contact her. I prayed constantly. After nine days there was a limited cease-fire. It was still very difficult for men to travel, but my sister was able to make the trip to check on Luna and her family. Later that day she returned to my apartment with the news that Luna and her family were safe.

"Good … ," I answered. "Did Luna tell you anything?"

"No," she replied.

I was anxiously waiting for any kind of information. I got nothing. Suddenly, I saw Luna coming in from the balcony! She had come with my sister to see me. My sister and Luna started laughing when they saw the stunned look on my face. Luna had been out there the whole time, listening to everything I was saying. She wanted to surprise me. She sat down and looked me straight in my eyes and said, "Open your bible to Genesis 24." She read. "Laban and Bethuel answered, 'This is from the Lord; we can say nothing to you one way or the other. Here is Rebekah. Take her and go and let her become the wife of your master's son as the Lord has directed.'" I looked at Luna. I knew what she was showing me, but I wanted to hear it from her own mouth. "My answer is 'Yes.'" She smiled with embarrassment. "You are a great woman," I said. "I would be the happiest man on earth to have you as my wife and partner." We prayed together for some time, asking God to bless this step we were taking.

Our culture requires parental permission for marriage. When I spoke with Luna's father he smiled and said, "My son, if the Lord says yes, no one else can say no. God bless you in your life together." He hugged me and expressed his love and respect for me. I felt like jumping out of my skin because I was so happy. I spoke next to the college principal and asked him to give a word of blessing at our engagement party. He, too, showed his approval and was happy for us. And, of course, my parents needed to hear the good news. Because there was still no phone service, my Sister Diana went to make the announcement. They were ecstatic!

Lebanese culture requires the man to buy jewelry for his bride in addition to the engagement ring. At the right time, God provided the money I needed. My mother and sisters joined Luna and I in choosing the ring and jewelry set that she liked. It is at the engagement party where we both put on our engagement rings. A toast was made declaring our engagement and an extravagant dinner was served. Finally we could go out together and be alone without any objection from anyone. It was a wonderful time in our lives, getting to know more about each other, sharing our past with all of the joys and sorrows. We prayed together often and talked about everything. The days at the Bible college seemed long because the rules forbade us speaking to each other even though we were engaged. We waited until the evenings to go out together and to be able to talk freely. I was so anxious to share every detail of my life with Luna. I found myself talking endlessly while she just sat and listened attentively. We prayed about all of our needs. One of the biggest was to know where God wanted us to live and serve him. We believed the Lord was leading us to Kafarshima where a ramshackle house next to the church kept us busy fixing up. This would become our first home and base of ministry.

Luna would be graduating in May, so we planned the wedding for July 1991. It was a busy time in our lives, but a very happy time. We chose the wedding invitations and spent evenings writing them. According to custom, we delivered them by hand. The wedding was like a dream. Luna was very beautiful and the sermon was exactly what we had prayed for. Many of our relatives had never attended a wedding outside of the Catholic Church and they were touched by both the ceremony and the message of Christ. Elie and Luna became one, Mr. and Mrs. Hasbani. We started our wonderful life as a married couple. I no longer served the Lord by myself. We were now serving the Lord together. We continue to hold fast the words of Jesus. "Haven't you read that at the beginning the Creator made them male and female. And for this reason a man will leave his father and mother and be united to his wife, and the two will become one flesh. So they are no longer two but one. Therefore, what God has joined together, let man not separate."

As we began our married life together, we were determined not to think of marriage and ministry as two mutually exclusive, often competing elements in our lives.

Rather, we worked to develop a perspective and practice that would see our marriage as the context and circumstance of our ministry together. We hoped to create a real experience where what was good for our marriage would empower our ministry; and what furthered our ministry would supply fulfillment in our marriage. We began our lives together never thinking our marriage must be a second priority to our ministry or that our ministry would take from the pleasure of marriage. As time has gone by and the family has grown, we have had the joy of discovering so many ways in which the strength of our marriage has enabled our ministry and the diligent work of ministry has fulfilled our mutual purpose as husband and wife. The more patriarchal character of the Middle Eastern culture in which we were living in Lebanon allowed Luna to create and manage a home that became a safe haven for a community of God's people and that same character required me to make certain her labors were not in vain.

Chapter 12
Ministry in Lebanon

Together, Luna and I made our marriage an instrument and our home a haven for kingdom work. As our family grew, even the children were included in the joy of serving the Lord. Our lives were filled with working for the Lord we loved. Lebanon and her varied peoples were near and dear to our hearts, so much so that perhaps we were beginning to forget our greater call to the nations.

I was not even 30 years old and already God had begun to fill my life with precious blessings and valuable lessons. The boy who had been immersed in the life and culture of his beloved homeland, Lebanon, was now experiencing a transforming power to change all of his desires and expectations. The patriotism for a country that promised me both the pleasures of life in the country and in a cosmopolitan setting was replaced, in the crucible of civil war and personal tragedy, with a devotion to the kingdom of Jesus and his love for the people of every language and nation. The sometime spoiled status as first-born son exposed less than noble character as I matured within the military setting. My cultural religion had left me empty and was unable to answer my questions or clear my conscience until, in a life and death drama, I established a personal relationship with Jesus Christ. My struggle to learn what it meant to follow Jesus and become his disciple after that drama had given me an entirely new perspective on the world around me. Enemies were now my brothers; humility was the way of exaltation; and obedience was the pathway of blessing. My newfound, now-found God had given me a new life that deservedly claimed all my energy and passion to serve him.

Now I had a wife who shared the same vision to share Jesus Christ with all the nations. Our starting point was my service as assistant pastor in the Church of God. In addition to that work, I was assigned to serve as pastor of a little house church in Kafarshima (just outside of Beirut). There had once been a fledgling group of believers who worshipped there, but the civil war had disrupted any progress. We would help them to once again reach out to their neighbors. It was there Luna and I made our first home. Our lives were filled with ministry, ministry, and more ministry! I continued working toward my theology degree at the Mediterranean Bible College. There were the monthly trips when I returned to the area of Deir Mimas in south Lebanon where I also continued to share the good news of Jesus.

These were exciting days as Luna and I learned how to work together and devote our little house to the purposes of God in a war-torn country in the Middle East. Everything looked so different to me as I learned to serve the body of Christ and at the same time to be responsible as the head of a household. Luna and I have different talents and gifts. Her work and prayer at home has been the basis for my ministry outside the home. It is always a blessing to return home in the evening, knowing that I have a place where I can find spiritual, physical, and emotional rest. Luna is also a prayer warrior. Early on in our marriage, we developed the practice of spending time daily reading the Bible and praying together.

One of the difficult lessons we had to learn early in our marriage and ministry together involved the openness of our home. It would have been easy to consider our house a retreat where we could close out the rest of the world and hide from it when we thought it too inconvenient to be open and available. God showed us, however, that our home needed to be open and welcoming. My experience with YWAM served us well during this time. It was there I had learned God was seeking individuals from all nations to worship him, even those I thought to be my enemy. By keeping our home open, we regularly found ourselves sharing the saving gospel of Jesus Christ to the many nationalities who were seeking answers to the questions life presents.

In addition to a weekly Bible study we held in our house, we also had a day just for prayer. All were invited to come and bring whatever spiritual or physical need they had so that we might pray with them. A Christian couple came to our home, desperately praying for a child. They had been married for several years, but were unable to conceive. We prayed with them and pleaded with God to answer the desire of their heart. They were soon blessed with a healthy baby girl.

We also opened our home daily for a leadership training school. This was called the 'Joshua Mission School' and was a joint effort of the Church of God and Youth With A Mission. This was a very difficult decision to make. We had to be ready by 8:00 AM to welcome all the students, serve them breakfast, as well as lunch; teach and care for them until late in the afternoon. Luna and I prayed before making this commitment and together we knew God wanted it. We saw God's hand and presence daily in our home…healing, reviving, reconciling, and blessing not only us, but also all who entered our home.

One summer, we opened our home on a grand scale for two weeks. A large group of Christian youth came from different Arab countries to participate in a gathering called "Love Lebanon," a conference and training session sponsored by Operation Mobilization (OM) and a number of area churches. About ten young people stayed in our home. During the day, I would take the youth out to share the gospel message while Luna would stay home to make meals and do all the work necessary to care for these workers. One day during this outreach ministry a family welcomed us into their home. As I shared about Jesus, I sensed in my heart that this family was passing through some difficult time. "Is there anyone sick in the family?" I asked. "I would like to pray for him." Quickly the wife rushed inside one of the bedrooms and came back holding a nine-month old child. "My son has leukemia!" she cried in desperation. I asked her if I could hold the baby. And I began to pray. As I did, both of the parents fell to their knees and started weeping for their salvation and for the healing of their sick child. The presence of the Lord was strong in the room. God not only healed the child, but he also saved the parents.

When I returned home late that night and shared with Luna what had happened, I had a joy that I had not felt in a long time. In the middle of the night, I had a terrifying dream. Four devils were holding me tightly to the bed and choking me so that I couldn't breathe. I tried to speak or scream, but couldn't. I was trying to call out Jesus' name, but

I was not able to say it out loud. Luna heard me moaning, trying to say something, and choking on my own words. She quickly realized that it was an attack from Satan. She started praying for me and shouting out the name of Jesus. Instantly, I felt released from their grip and I joined in shouting out the name of the Lord. "Jesus, Jesus, Jesus!" Luna and I prayed long into the night, proclaiming the protection found through the blood of Jesus over our family and over every part of our house and property. We asked for God's protection; we surrendered our family and all our possessions into His hands. We included in our prayers the community around us, asking God to protect them, as well, from the attacks of these evil spirits.

We were encouraged by all the aspects of ministry in which we were involved. The results were exciting, but the spiritual battles were great. These battles came through parts of the Christian population who were deep in bondage to ancient traditions that seemed to be century old shackles of lifeless rituals of mostly cultural significance. There was also the darkness of Islam whose followers became increasingly more vicious in direct proportion to the measure of ignorance that engulfed them. Both groups are deeply loved by the Lord, but reaching them is very difficult because they believe they are secure by following a man-made and often politically motivated institution. I was again reminded that the spirit of ancient Phoenician Baal worship has lingered among some of the Arab population of Lebanon, keeping many in bondage to worshipping idols and statues in ritual forms and rites. Our hearts were broken for all, Muslim and Christian alike, desiring that they should find the true reason for living and the source of all life…Jesus!

During my training in the army, I was taught how to fight the enemy using fake weapons. Even though it was tough training, we knew the training period with an imaginary enemy would prepare us to face real weapons and real enemies. We often fired words instead of bullets shouting, "Fire, fire, fire!" When we finished training, we went out to the battlefield where the enemy was really firing at us and everything changed! Everything became painstakingly real. We had a real fear of making a mistake that could cost us our lives or the life of a friend. I began to view my spiritual life and my practical training in the same way. Everything was real now, not some idea or theory on paper. I started experiencing it as I practiced it. And this brought with a range of results from joy and sadness, success and failure, gentleness and toughness, love and hate, satisfaction and defeat. God was showing me biblical training and practical training are equally important and they complement one another.

These years of ministry in Lebanon were continually filled with incidents that affirmed my confidence in God's faithfulness. We should never doubt that he will be near to bless our efforts. During one ministry trip to the south of the country, a fellow believer approached me, asking if I would like some Bibles for distribution to the local villages. Of course I said yes, never expecting what I would find. Missionaries with The Voice of Hope in the early 1980's brought with them a treasure trove of Bibles. As we entered the house where this cache had been hidden for the past ten years of ethnic and religious fighting, I was shown to a room that was literally packed high and wide with 10,000 Bibles. I was stunned by gift this really was and went into action by assembling a ten-member team that fanned out into an area of approximately 15 villages and began to offer free Bibles to Muslims and Christians alike. To our amazement our reception was great. The Middle East TV station had already touched the hearts and minds of so many that they were eager to be given the Christian scriptures so they could read them for themselves. This was just another example to us of the providence of God in reaching out to all people, including those still in the darkness and bondage of Islam.

In the midst of all this, there was also the joy of family life. In 1992, Luna gave birth to our first son. We named him David to remind us of the anointing on our lives even as King David had enjoyed the anointing of God for his life and ministry. I have always had a special place in my heart for that great king whose life so influenced by own spiritual growth. His life was a picture of contrasts: lowly shepherd and yet a king; sensitive poet, but also fearless warrior; beloved of Jonathan, but hated by King Saul; and a frightful enemy of the Philistines and also their ally. God gave me a dream one night. I found myself wandering in an ancient palace until I reached a room with an old man seated in a royal chair. Ten counselors sat before him and he invited me to sit with the rest. "I am David," he said. "Very few people have the chance to sit and listen to my voice and hear my teaching. I want you to be wise, Elie. Walk by the anointing of the Holy Spirit in your life. Be obedient and faithful to the calling in your life. Come near to me." And he blessed me saying, "I love you. I want you to set me before you as an example. Remember these verses: Does the Lord really want sacrifices and offerings? No, he doesn't want your sacrifices. He wants you to obey him. Rebelling against God or disobeying him because you are proud is just as bad as worshiping idols or asking them for advice." I awoke ecstatic. We would name our first son David ("The Loved One") as a constant reminder of that anointing in our lives.

I learned early as a father how even a small child can lead and teach us. I was preparing a sermon on faith early one morning, working in my small study at home in Kafarshima. David came running into my study, wanting to play. I picked him up and amused him for a brief time, but because I had important things to get done, I sent him out of the room and closed the door, calling to Luna to keep him from disturbing me any more. He started crying and pounding at the door, wanting to come in and play with me some more. I was trying to ignore him and was somewhat irritated by his incessant knocking and calling out to me. Finally, I jumped up and went to the door. As I opened it, his face lit up with joy and excitement as he ran into the room and took his place on my chair, ready for some more fun. Just as I was going to be angry and call for Luna, the Holy Spirit spoke to my heart, "Elie, that is faith!" David believed I was in the room; he believed I would open the door; he believed I was a loving father. Spiritual truths often come through our children if we're willing to listen.

Our second son was born in 1995. In the seventh month, serious problems developed and the doctor insisted she have total bed rest. He was very concerned that a premature birth would be harmful or fatal for the child. Luna and I drew very close as we asked God to protect our child. We spent time reading the scriptures together and became convinced God intended to give us this child when we read in Isaiah 66. "Do I bring to the moment of birth and not give delivery? Says the

Lord. Do I close up the womb when I bring to delivery? Says your God." God kept that promise to us and gave us a healthy baby boy. We named him Daniel John.

As our family grew in size and as our needs increased, it was tempting to close out the rest of the world and focus on what was most precious to me. God reminded us again about the purpose of the family so we began to teach our children as they were growing up that they, too, were part of the ministry to the nations and to share with all people the good news of Jesus. Sometimes we would plan family outings with the purpose of distributing Bibles and Christian pamphlets about Jesus and his saving work toward Muslims. God often used the boys more than he used us as people gladly received what they had to share about salvation. It was amazing to watch because the simplicity of the children was so attractive to so many; they were more eager to listen and receive from them than from adults. We invited many to our home and a few of them also came for Sunday worship services.

In this setting with my growing family, the church in our home at Kafarshima was also beginning to grow and we were becoming rooted in our ministry in Lebanon. It was exciting to see the effects of our work as the teaching to forgive enemies and to share the good news of Jesus with all people were included in our daily ministry. Cultural Christians from among the national population of Lebanon and God-fearing Muslims were responding to the message of God's kingdom in Jesus Christ. We experienced many spiritual battles as the word of God confronted the spiritual and political hornets nest of the Middle East region. There were challenges as we worked to incorporate our family life with the ministry centered in our home, but bringing light to Lebanon was near to our hearts and we gained valuable lessons as we continued on in ministry.

God began opening new doors of ministry for me in the area of reconciliation ministry, between Arabs and Jews, and Christians of many nationalities still separated as enemies by ethnic and cultural differences. This work took me on trips to many countries…Cyprus, Turkey, Jordan, and others. Travel to Israel had to be done by way of Cyprus or via the SLA controlled security/buffer zone in south Lebanon that I had helped to defend. Often Hezbollah radicals forbidding travel to Israel closed that route. Once in Israel, I was able to travel and minister, working with Messianic Jews, Arab Christians, and Muslim converts. Meetings of Musalaha (Arabic for forgiveness and reconciliation) were organized to bring Christians of different national and religious backgrounds together in peace and love. One of the very precious memories I have of those meetings was of an Arab brother who accepted my invitation to come with me. His anxious outburst in anticipation of the event betrayed the misunderstanding and darkness that characterizes the mindset of many in the Middle East. "What are you doing to me, Elie? Do you think I can meet a Jew? I never met one before. What do they look like? Are you trying to get me killed? I know I will never forgive a Jew. I am afraid to meet them. What do I have to say to them? I never heard of a good Jew in my country." There was a great deal of fear and stress as he rambled on and on. "What will happen to me if my government finds out that I actually met an Israeli? I will never get out of jail. Maybe no one will work with me anymore or my ministry will be in danger. And nobody will trust me ever again!" During that reconciliation meeting, as former enemies found common grounds for peace in Jesus Christ, I watched the expression of amazement come over his face when his heart and mind suddenly opened to the possibility of having unity in Jesus with someone he thought an enemy. Later, as we left the conference, he thanked me for the invitation that brought him to a place of peace, release, and blessing. He had come to a much greater understanding of the breadth and depth of God's love for all people. Within months, I could see his ministry rapidly growing. "If I can love my enemies, the Jews, then I can easily forgive those who sin against me from among the Arabs!" A *musalaha* had taken place in his life and it was now easy to see the peace of God on his face. God was at work reconciling believers of many national and religious backgrounds, bringing them together in peace and love.

These were very busy and exciting times as we saw the ministry expanding and bearing much fruit for the Lord. We were focused on the work and so excited to be a part of what God was doing. Perhaps we were too content. Perhaps we were even losing the vision for the nations that God had given me during my time in Cyprus. But God was about to remind us of the call and give us a new direction of obedience. It would take time for us to fully be persuaded and for God to work out the details, but he had new plans on the horizon.

PART V
MISSIONARIES IN THE USA

Chapter 13
Transitional Period

We began to sense a call to the United States. I would feel the sting of being stripped by God of all the wonderful earthly blessings he had given. The ministry in Lebanon, my wife and sons, our home and friends would all need to be yielded to the Lord as the calling to be his disciple and to follow him once again changed the course of my life. Would Jesus be enough?

One day, as Luna and I were at home praying and seeking the Lord's purposes in our lives, I felt directed to look at a world map I had hanging on the wall. The Lord was speaking to me through the Holy Spirit and it was awesome what I was hearing. God was saying our calling was not just to serve him in Lebanon with the work of preaching, teaching, and reconciliation there. He reminded me of the first vision he had given me. From the very beginning of my walk with him, he was calling me to proclaim the Good News to all the nations. I felt a sense of renewal in this call and I felt that Jesus now wanted to move us to the United States. While I had always respected America and been impressed with her place in the world, it was difficult for me to comprehend, even to believe the sense of drawing I was experiencing. Luna was sensing the same message from the Lord. We continued in prayer, knowing we would need God's wisdom to understand this new and unexpected calling. During these times of prayer, I felt an almost personal word of encouragement and calling as I read Ephesians 2:12-15:

> ...remember that at that time you were separate from Christ, excluded from citizenship in Israel and foreigners to the covenants of the promise, without hope and without God in the world. But now in Christ Jesus you who once were far away have been brought near by the blood of Christ.

> Christ broke down the walls of separation and enmity between different people groups through his finished work on the cross. We would need to wait patiently on the Lord in order to learn how all the details of such a calling could come to pass.

Our situation in Lebanon was growing increasingly more difficult and dangerous. How could we share where we believed God's was leading us without our being understandably accused of "jumping ship," of not being willing to do the Lord's work in a difficult place and at a difficult time? I was convinced that everyone would laugh at us and criticize us. And that is exactly what happened. Some said that the United States would be the last place to which God would call us. Others said we were running away from our true calling. And still others looked at us as worldly people going after the material things available in the United States. Some well-meaning people said, "Why would God call you to a place that has no need? No region has greater needs than the Middle East!" But we continued to pray, looking toward the Lord to lead us by faith.

It occurred to me that if God was indeed leading us toward the United States, then perhaps I should make a type of reconnaissance trip there. Even getting a tourist visa seemed an insurmountable task. When I was in Cyprus for one of the reconciliation meetings, I decided to give God another opportunity to confirm for me that I was rightly sensing his leading. I went to the American embassy there and applied for that hard to get visa. Much to my amazement, it was granted to me. So it was that I took a first step by visiting the United States in 1997.

I admit that all of my motives were not so pure. Many of my expectations were uninformed and I was quite unprepared for so many things this "discovery" trip would reveal to me. For one thing, American prosperity is coveted and much abused by many in the world. Even Christians in other lands often think of the church in the United States as the cash cow to provide for them. I, too, thought that perhaps I would be able to raise further support as I made this trip. Visiting the United States was like a fantastic dream come true. I grew up wondering what a land of constitutional law based on the Bible might really be like. This was the land of my childhood imagination where there was peace and prosperity. One of my first surprises was the sheer size of a land with 9.83 million km^2. I got maps and studied them. A trip of a few hours had been a long journey in my experience, but here, a plane trip of a few hours only got me a very short distance in the expanse of the United States.

Other things were more troubling as I made this first visit in the United States. I traveled to eight different states during my visit and discovered to my great surprise a profound need among the people to hear the gospel. From our perspective in the Middle East, we assumed the United States was a blessed land because of its faithfulness to Christ, but I discovered the West's division between church and state created a gaping chasm of secular thinking and pagan living that not only divided the people of the nation, but also left deep scars of worldliness in the church itself. I was surprised at the number of denominations and independent congregations that made up the fabric of Christianity. The importance and independence of the individual to the United States psyche were almost shocking. I learned the need of the nations for King Jesus was as great in the United States as it was in the war torn Middle East.

When I returned to Lebanon and the ministry there, Luna and I felt that God was continuing to confirm we would be moving as a family to the United States in the near future. Considering all of the language, cultural, and political roadblocks, this seemed like a fantastic dream, but I was very eager now for God to open the next doors of our nations ministry in his timing and in his way. This he did by beginning to close the doors of the ministry in Lebanon. My background as a member of the South Lebanese Army and my previous involvement with the reconciliation ministry in the Middle East between Arabs and Jews (which included visiting the off-limits country of Israel) all worked together to make me increasingly a persona non-gratis in my own home country. By 1999, I was feeling tremendous pressure from the fanatic Hezbollah Muslims, as well as from the Syrian-controlled Lebanese government. My cousin, who was a major in the Lebanese Army, had access to information that he shared with me: Hezbollah was watching me and gathering information that could end in my imprisonment or even murder.

One of the closed doors hurt me deeply. I was denied ordination by the area council of the Church of God. This rejection was a very painful disappoint for me. I had completed my studies at the Mediterranean Bible College; I was now married to a daughter of a faithful member of the church; and I myself had served for years in the ministry of the church. When the day came for my examination for ordination before the area council, I thought I was prepared in every way necessary. I was able to adequately answer all of the theological questions about the basics of the Christian faith, the doctrines of the Trinity, the cross, the nature of Jesus Christ, and the gifts of the Holy Spirit as taught by the Church of God. At the close of the examination I shared again my personal testimony and my vision for the nations. I told them of the work of reconciliation and also mentioned the opposition I was facing from Hezbollah. I was sent outside the room to wait for the council's decision. I was confident of their approval; obviously, I was a proper candidate for ordination as proven by my many years of service. When I was invited back into the room an hour later, I sensed in their stares that something was amiss. The head of the council began by commending me, praising my work and my doctrine. I had passed the test, he said, BUT the council felt that it was not a good time to give official ordination papers because of the political dangers surrounding my past and my visits to Israel in the work of reconciliation. The council felt the safety of both my family and the church membership required me to leave the country as soon as possible. They would give me a certification, allowing a church in that unknown host country to officially ordain me in the Church of God, but that was all. I was shocked. I was very disappointed and suffered the deep hurt of rejection. These were the people I loved and worked together with for the Lord. Luna and I determined to see this painful experience as the hand of God working out a greater plan. We had been rejected by our homeland and now by our church co-workers, but our God had not reject us. We would wait on God, trusting his wisdom and goodness.

Wearing a clerical collar on many occasions gave me a certain amount of protection because of the general deference shown in the Middle East to religious persons, but the rising political tensions along with my past military history and my present work of Christian evangelizing all began to take their toll on my ability to minister safely in Lebanon. Now all my family and friends were urging me to leave not just for my own safety, but also for the safety of my wife and children. With the refusal of my ordination, my spiritual leaders and co-workers, who previously thought I was forsaking the work, all advised me to leave the country. This proved to be wise counsel and the providential goodness of God.

It was clear to me the situation in Lebanon was dangerous. That God was leading us to the United States was also very clear to Luna and me. While God had provided something of a vision and seemed to be forcing the issue through circumstances, many of the details were not so obvious. Because of the pressures from Hezbollah and the added concern of family and friends, I once again thought it best to make a trip to the United States. I still had my temporary visa for the United States, but my family had no documentation for travel. I would need to leave them behind once again. So on a spring evening, I boarded a plane at the Beirut airport and said goodbye to Luna, our two little boys, David and Danny, and a few close family members. People were simple told I would be traveling, visiting my sister, Diana, who had moved with her family to Michigan. Only close family and congregation members knew the real reason I was leaving. In my mind, I was still only making a tactical ministry retreat. I convinced myself I would return to continue serving the church in Lebanon when the political tensions eased and life there returned to normal.

When I was alone on the plane, I finally had time to seriously consider the situation in Lebanon, the separation from my family, and my ministry. All of it began to greatly trouble me. The uncertainties surrounding my departure were all I could think about. By the time I arrived at the airport in Detroit and met Diana, my struggles overwhelmed me and I sat on the curbside sobbing. "I feel like I lost everything. I don't know where I am going from here." It was May 19, 1999. Indeed, it was an overwhelming sense of loss and uncertainty because of the circumstances surrounding my leaving Lebanon and the concern for my family. I was forced during these days to face very personal questions about the cost of discipleship. I was pressured to embrace the call to follow Jesus even if it meant the loss of my homeland, family, and even visions of ministry. Days of prayer and encouragement from family helped to temporarily lift my spirits. I decided to call Dr. Marc Erickson, Senior Pastor of Eastbrook Church in Milwaukee, Wisconsin. I had first met him in Lebanon where he and his congregation were involved in various Middle Eastern ministries. He was personally acquainted with Lucien Accad, head pastor of our church in Mansourieh. Marc had heard me share my testimony and showed an interest in my vision and ministry work. I had called him before leaving Lebanon and he had invited me to visit his church saying, "We'll see where it goes from there."

As it happened, the Ericksons had a wedding to attend in Michigan. They made room in their car for me and we returned to Milwaukee together. In their home, I was made to feel extremely welcome by their Christian love and hospitality. Marc invited me to visit Eastbrook Church where I met many people involved in missions. The believers were truly interested in praying for the spread of the gospel to all the nations of the world. Marc, his wife Nancy, and church members helped me to adjust and feel welcome. My emotions were still volatile as my mind and heart were still in Lebanon with family and ministry. I was safe and happy here. My lovely wife and two little boys were still there. I began to worry that I would never see them again. It was impossible for them to come to the United States.

As my situation was discussed with more people, someone suggested that I should go back to school and finish my master's degree at Trinity International University. If accepted into the program at Trinity I would be issued an I-20 form that would allow me to get an F-1 student visa and Luna and the children would qualify for an F-2 visa. I could study here and my family could join me. Obviously, I was very excited about this possibility. A visit to Trinity, however, quickly turned to disillusionment when I learned of the requirements. It would be necessary for me to pass the TOEFL (Test of English as a Foreign Language) test. I would also need to get transcripts of all my grades from Lebanon. All of these requirements would take many months at the best. In addition to all of these obstacles was the cost of tuition…$15,000! Both my English language skills and my financial situation seemed to be dead end roadblocks to any thought of my doing further schooling.

I returned to the Erickson's gravely disappointed. In the privacy of my room I cried hard and decided before God, "Lord, I'm going back home unless you do something! I don't care if I live or die. There is no reason to stay. Everything tells me I don't belong here." In desperation, I decided to fast, pray, and study the Scriptures for three days in hopes of receiving clarity concerning the Lord's will. Over the days he encouraged me with many scripture passages, cautioning me not to forget His promises. The clarity I was longing for came unmistakably when I physically heard the Lord say loudly, "I will bring your family here in one month." God was promising so much. My prayer now became a cry that God would confirm for me the desire of my heart. The work would continue, not in Lebanon, but in the United States. And he would do it by accomplishing another *impossible thing*… bringing my family to be with me within a month of my own arrival.

I called Luna immediately. I instructed her to start selling our belongings and to prepare herself and the children to come to the United States. I even told her to book airline tickets. We would proceed on faith. Amazingly Luna did everything I told her to do! Luna began selling things as I asked. When she shared with our pastor in Lebanon what we were doing and what all needed to happen, he warned her that it was impossible for such things to happen so quickly. She responded that she would do what I asked and when she even began getting rid of household items Lucien said, "You're nuts!" Filled with confidence from the Lord, I told Marc I wanted to go back to Trinity and try again. This time I assured the dean that I would work to pass the TOEFL exam. God favored me in their eyes and I was accepted. But even I was startled and humbled when I learned that Eastbrook Church would provide the funds for my tuition. God was using the church in America to further his purposes for my own life. And disciples such as Marc Erickson were diligent and gracious to use their gifts and experience to accomplish his will. I never would have been able to work my way through the many technicalities alone, but these Christian friends knew the "ropes" and were able to make the necessary contacts to bring it all together. This new family at Eastbrook knew how to pray.

Back in Lebanon, Lucien's brother Philip Accad, having American citizenship and contacts at the US embassy in Beirut, took up the cause for Luna and the boys. As soon as the necessary forms from Trinity University had been forwarded to Lebanon, he rushed them to the embassy. Two days before her flight was to leave for the US, Luna received her visa. I had arrived in the United States on May 19th. Luna, David, and Danny arrived on June 18th. Just as God had promised when I heard his voice while fasting, my family was with me in the United States within a month's time of my own arrival. This confirmed to our family that our God is the God of the impossible and we had heard him correctly concerning his leading.

We were now safely in the United States, just in time. When in 2000 the IDF withdrew from southern Lebanon, the SLA disintegrated and dangerous times followed for Christians and former members of the SLA. Its members either surrendered to Hezbollah or the Lebanese army, or returned quietly to their villages. Others sought emergency relief with their families in Israel. Military courts in Beirut sentenced hundreds of SLA members to prison terms ranging from months to years for collaborating with the enemy. SLA commanders tried in absentia received death sentences. Others fled as refugees to other parts of the world, seeking to make a new life. The emotional scars remain for many who loved and fought for their country only to be hated and turned away in disgrace.

My own extended family has experienced the painful loss of our Lebanese homeland. The pleasant memories of life in Deir Mimas seem a distant history colored by a tinge of painful regret. My parents are refugees in the United States; several sisters and a brother have fled to Israel to establish new lives; and another brother has also immigrated to the United States. How true it is that we are pilgrims and strangers on this earth where we have no continuing city. The story of our family has been repeated thousands of times over as Jews, Christians, and Muslims alike suffer the painful consequences of sin and the wars of mankind.

God continued to show in every way that floods of blessing would follow our little steps of obedience. God gave us grace in the eyes of many and gifts began to pour in…an apartment, living expenses, a car, food, and help in adjusting to our new surroundings. There were continuous challenges related to the language, culture, and especially my studies, but minute by minute we felt God's assurance and His peace. It was now our turn as a family to obey the

Lord by learning to follow his directions and endure the struggles of learning to live in a new country and a different culture. It would be up to God's faithfulness to make the way of ministry plain before us.

Chapter 14
Life in the USA

God had moved us to the United States and provided in remarkable ways. The joy of having me family together in the safety of a new location was contrasted with the demands of adjusting to a new culture and fulfilling the commitments of additional schooling. Gradually I would come to accept that God had now closed my ministry door in Lebanon and moved me to finish my academic study and onto a new field of labor!

Elie, Luna and their boys David, Daniel and Joseph

The book of Acts in the Bible tells the story of the early church being forced out of Jerusalem by persecution resulting in becoming the first missionaries. Wherever they went they began to proclaim the good news of Jesus. We are not told about their fears and discomforts, which must have been many. We are simply told that they fled for their lives and their difficulties became the occasion for the advance of the church. Looking back, Luna and I realize our experience was very much the same. It was an unplanned and uncomfortable disruption of our lives, including dangers from malevolent powers of religion and government that God used to push us out of Lebanon and overseas to the United States of America. Our departure was surrounded with challenges and uncertainties, but those very experiences would lay the groundwork for our part in spreading the gospel. Without our realizing it at the time, we were in effect becoming missionaries to internationals in the West. Of course at the time, we could only see the immediate problems that confronted us, but the Lord was focused on a much better goal and we trusted his leading.

Missionaries know, as they enter a foreign field, the first and often most disheartening experience is the overwhelming task of confronting culture shock. It requires making adjustments in order to live and to minister in what is to them a very strange world. All this must be done in the context of having been separated from all the normal supports of life…family, friends, language, and deeply rooted social customs. Luna and I faced these same demands to adapt as we entered the very strange and frenetically paced world of almost twenty-first century western civilization in the United States. Almost like little children, we became dependent on others in order to learn the basics of how to navigate in a new culture. This was a frightening and at times very humbling experience. It was only through the gracious love and support of God's people at Eastbrook Church that we were able to slowly succeed in taking the necessary steps to order our lives according to the demands of my continuing education and the challenges of grafting our family into what was for us a new world.

Day by day, slowly and painfully in many ways, we began to make a transition to a new life in a new land. Some of the more simple tasks of life became major stumbling blocks as we learned to live in an English-speaking environment and to navigate in a culture that was a sea of unfamiliar customs and strange cultural norms. Where does one go to buy groceries? How do you pay for them? An American supermarket does not function like the local vendors in an open-air public square of the Middle East! How do I get a car, a license, and gasoline for the car? What are the laws for driving? What do I say should I be stopped by the police? Why are Americans so individualistically minded? What does a shared life in community look like with a Christian congregation whose members have a Western worldview?

As we look back on those days of adjustment, we can now laugh with our friends, but at the time, many of these adjustments were painful. Life can be difficult when navigating in a new language, facing the intensity and sophistication of a country that has raced ahead of much of the world in technology, commerce, and modernity. We were often left feeling inferior and ashamed because of our background. The fear of the unknown often made us hesitant to try something new, knowing it would expose our sense of awkwardness and feelings of inadequacy. These experiences turned out to be wonderful! God would use them in the future when we began to minister to the internationals brought into our lives later. We would be able to understand their struggles that would challenge and hurt them.

The wonderful friends and growing relationships of our new church home at Eastbrook helped us to face the road ahead. We learned the difference between a grocery store and a mall. We began to make sense of all these names—JC Penny, K-Mark, Wal-Mart, Kohl's, Pick & Save, and so many more. We were given help with finances, postal services, tipping, the Internet, finding doctors and other medical assistance…the daily tasks of life that are often taken for granted. We had been the leaders, teachers, and guides in Lebanon, but here, we were the ones in need. We had to change our mindset and become the learners and not the teachers; but as we submitted to this new and often humbling position, we began to benefit from the help and ministry being offered to us. The sense that God had called us and was leading us on this journey by his Holy Spirit always gave life and fresh encouragement to the challenges we faced.

My first major task was to fulfill my responsibilities as a student of Trinity International University. Some things were minor adjustments, such as learning to drive on snow and ice. The 45-minute commute from home to class was inconvenient; several times the car broke down. Other adjustments required real effort. The professors assumed I understood everything in spite of my poor English. In reality, I probably understood less than half of what they were teaching! I compensated by reading more outlines and books. Luna was also a big help.

My second language at home had been French; hers had been English. She helped me to understand many things, translating and correcting my writing. All of this she did while keeping a house with small children and making her own adjustments in a new land. For both of us, the United States' culture of individualism, prosperity, and overly busy lives were the most difficult adjustments. I was challenged, but not anxious. It seemed to me that the blessings of life in the United State were so great that everything was easy when compared to the situations in Lebanon.

Doctoral Graduation 2009

We continued to seek God for the more specific purpose he had for bringing my family and me to the United States while we were making these adjustments in life. We knew he wanted us to serve the nations, but where and how? As I prayed and watched for open doors, I visited Arab congregations around the country. These were small immigrant groups for whom the struggle to survive spiritually, culturally, and financially was the extent of their vision. Their integration into American society came down to nothing more than the prosperity view of the American dream. They had no vision for anything beyond themselves. Their struggle to adapt to a new life and their desire to send support to family in their native lands left them with neither the interest, nor the time, nor the resources to share God's love with others. God seemed to close all of these doors so we continued to watch and pray for his leading.

While I was working on my master's degree, my family and I were working our way into the life of Eastbrook Church. These were the saints who had hosted us; they were the instruments God used to begin working out the details of our calling to the nations. They continue even now to be very dear to us. In 2001, I started to lead a Bible study for internationals. During the course of this study, I was especially drawn to the Old Testament story of Joseph. I was particularly struck by the way he embraced his sufferings. He became a well-adjusted, successful citizen in the foreign land of Egypt. Joseph was an encouraging example for me.

Our new life would include the addition of another child, our third. We were thinking of names beginning with the letter 'D' since it would correspond to the names of our first two sons, but before we had made a decision, Luna told me God had given her a dream in which she saw herself holding another baby boy and he gave her instructions to name him Joseph and so we did. He is a constant reminder to our family of the encouraging example God gave us in the Bible and that he blesses during hard times. The English name, Joseph, is in Hebrew, *Jussive*, from the verb *Yassap* which means "to add." God was surely adding blessing upon blessing for my family and others through the hardships we experienced. Just as God had brought Joseph to Egypt to be a blessing for others, so God had brought us to the United States; here he would bless us and here he would use us to be a blessing to others.

The events of September 11, 2001 affected our comfort and sense of being accepted; we were, after all, Arab immigrants from the Middle East. We knew our Christian community loved us, but when we were outside our Christian setting, did we need to explain to others who we were, where we were from, and that we were Christians? Because of my accent, I was hesitant to even speak. One moment I had felt so free and safe living in the United States and then all of a sudden I didn't even know if people would trust me. They seemed quite uninformed about the Middle East and Lebanon. Suddenly, I sensed danger just as I had at home in Lebanon.

God would also use September 11th to broaden the worldview of Christians around the world. It would no longer be possible to ignore the challenge of the hundreds of millions of Muslims in the world. The church would be compelled to face the realities of globalization which include God's universal intentions for his kingdom and his desire that his disciples become disciple-makers among the multi-ethnic peoples with whom they brush elbows daily. It became clear to us that these changes would further our calling and ministry to the nations.

Clearly God had been laying a great deal of groundwork to support our calling. As the studies at Trinity came to an end and I received my master's degree in 2002, I sought God's leading regarding the next move in my journey. God seemed to have opened no doors among Arab immigrant churches. I prayed that God would help me exercise my gifts: discipling new believers; reaching internationals, here temporarily as students or as business people, in their needs as I had personally come to understand them; and equipping the church to reach the nations. When it came right down to it, I felt I was already in the right place, Eastbrook Church. This congregation already had a good perspective of the church being a multi-ethnic gathering so it seemed the ideal place to take my next steps in ministry. Fortunately, the leadership felt the same and offered me a position on staff. I was ordained by the church and became the Pastor to the Nations. This ministry would come to have two prongs: First, to equip the church to serve in ministry locally; and, second, to reach out in love to internationals here temporarily (students and professionals) and permanently (refugees and immigrants) in order to befriend them and share the gospel. With these two approaches also came the responsibility to nurture and support new believers by assimilating them into the larger church body, promoting interaction and cultural understanding within the church. This is no small vision. The interaction and cultural understanding can only happen with the help of God and a humble and willing-to-learn attitude on the part of the people.

Launching this nations ministry has been both exciting and challenging. Many believers do have a sincere heart for to reach those from different cultures, but the church in the United States also has many stumbling blocks created by the culture of the society. While the people are very friendly, they are also fiercely independent. As a result they are not as committed to the family and the community as in the Middle Eastern culture in which I was raised. They are outstanding in organizing and planning agendas, but most become so busy there is little time to follow through on those plans. Every culture has its own strengths and weaknesses. I had to learn to be aware of this and sensitive to all in my new position. It was a process and at times stressful. Problems always fall on the leader and this ministry was no different. The leader is on the front line, even the front line of judgments. Sometimes the leader is even viewed as the problem, not as the solution! So in spite of my eagerness to get the Nations Ministry of Eastbrook Church established, there were more struggles in doing so than I anticipated.

In my heart, there still lingered a special love for the Middle East and especially for Lebanon. I wondered if God intended all of my new knowledge and experience to be used in my homeland; that perhaps the move to the United States was merely a temporary one. As the oldest son, I still had responsibilities to my family. The expectation that I should continue to help the entire family only became more intense when I became a pastor. I was expected to 'save' the family financially and spiritually whether they lived in Lebanon or in the United States. I wanted to help in every situation, but I simply was not able to do so. It was difficult sometimes to even think of helping while I was dealing with my own struggle to build a new ministry and care for my young family. As long as I trusted in faith, God provided gifts for my use. I was confident I was doing what God wanted of me, but I wanted to be open to possible changes.

In 2005, Eastbrook Church gave me an opportunity to test the waters of change by attending a mission conference in Egypt with two other congregational leaders. After the conference, we visited sister churches of Eastbrook in Jordan and Lebanon. It was encouraging for me to see how God continued to be at work in the Middle East. I was excited when it was time to proceed to Lebanon, the land of my birth. This was where I lived most of my life, lost part of my leg, accepted Christ, served the church, and discipled others. God spoke to me in this land and gave me his vision. This was my land. I was coming back. I was filled with exuberant and melancholic emotions as our plane landed at the Beirut airport.

Things went wrong quickly, however. My traveling companions, from United States, were allowed entry, but I was stopped and detained. The government agents were rude and disrespectful, grabbing my passport and visa, telling me to send my traveling companions on without me while I was ordered to get my bags and follow them. I was placed under arrest and taken for interrogation. My name was on a wanted list because of my past connections to the SLA. After lengthy questioning about my travels to Israel and past involvement in the SLA, I was told that I would be allowed one call. It was then I remembered I had a clerical collar in my suitcase. Hoping the respect accorded clergy might better my predicament, I asked if I could freshen up and change my clothing. When I returned to the interrogation room wearing the clerical collar, the entire atmosphere changed. Now the guard's first questions were about my clergy credentials and my ministerial service. Suddenly they showed respect and civility in their dealings with me. I made a call to my cousin who was a major in the Lebanese army and told him what had happened. He assured me that he would go to work as quickly as possible to see how he could get my name removed from all of the offending lists, but this would take days and there was no way I would be able to be released until all of the databases could be changed. That night I was jailed with six Muslim men. When they saw my clerical collar, they were filled with respectful questions about Christ, the Bible, and Christianity. I had to be careful to hide my prosthesis in order to avoid political discussions, but I spent the night like the jailed apostle Paul, witnessing to Christ and his gift. By morning all six men had heard the gospel and one accepted Christ!

The next morning I was handcuffed and removed from the jail cell. I was told that my passport would be held until my name had been deleted from the wanted list of all four of Lebanon's security departments. My visit to Lebanon was certainly turning out to be very different than expected. The process of purging my name from the security computer lists took more than a week, but with the help of relatives and by the prayers of the saints, the difficult task was completed. As soon as I received my passport back, I left Lebanon. God had been at work behind the scenes by having just the right person in a place of authority at the right time. Only the future will tell if God has other long-range plans to be accomplished by clearing my name from security lists in Lebanon.

Perhaps the more important lesson gained from my aborted attempt to once again visit and minister in my beloved homeland of Lebanon is what I call my own personal Jonah experience. While I had come to deeply appreciate God's work in bringing my family and me to minister to the nations in the United States, I had harbored a desire to minister in the Middle East. This inner attitude of resistance to the plan of God in my life had been, without my truly realizing it, very much like Jonah getting aboard a ship to flee from God's direction to go to Nineveh. My hesitancy to fully embrace ministry in the United States and let go of the vision of ministry in Lebanon was displeasing to God. As I sat in a filthy Beirut jail for those nights, I began to contemplate some of the ways Jonah must have been thinking for his duration in the belly of a whale. Had these miserable surroundings been caused by my desire to minister in a time and place God had not directed? Was there perhaps even a rebellion against God's word to me and my calling to follow him? In the words of the prophet, does God desire obedience or sacrifice? I spent much time during those days searching my own thoughts and heart. When I was 'vomited' out on the shore some days later, it was with a chastened heart that I returned to the United States and the work of ministry to the nations at Eastbrook.

I had come to America as an international student. As such I often felt out of place, alone, and anxious about the many cultural changes around me. While these times were difficult and often unpleasant, God needed me to experience them so I could better understand the people of other cultures he would bring into my life. To be a missionary one has to give up a portion of his own uniqueness in order to relate to those he is serving. I needed to become an international in order to reach internationals. I needed to suffer loneliness in order to help those feeling isolated and alone. I needed to feel anxious in order to be a comfort to others who were experiencing the same. Jesus himself was tempted in everyway and so understands our weaknesses. God would use all I had experienced for the work he gave me at Eastbrook. Nothing was lost.

Chapter 15
Hope Continues

God has freed me from many of the narrow views of my childhood, breaking down many of the constricting walls of my youth and planting in my heart a love and a vision for all nations. Slowly, we have realized God is keeping His promised vision to us in a unique way; we have indeed become missionaries to internationals in the United States.

As these pages go to print, I have the exciting sense that God is on the move, both in the world and in my own life. On the larger scene of the world, God is plainly at work accomplishing his eternal purposes and we are able only to stand back in awe, watching as his every word is accomplished; his every promise is fulfilled. The "gates of hell" will not be able to resist his building program for the church. The battle is at times bloody and the enemies of God are powerful, but the extremes of the frightening process only prove the certainty of his victory. On a personal level, you can rejoice with me that so much of God's grace has already been fulfilled in my life. The former spoiled boy from Lebanon, who did not really know God, has come a long way! From the cloistered walls of my youth, God has brought me to understand and to appreciate his heart for all people and nations. Together, with my wife and my family, we sense that God has removed us from our little corner of the world to share the message of God's inner peace for all who will hear and follow him. Our flight from the tragedy and danger of Lebanon was God's way of providing us with a base camp to the nations here in the United States. It is from this God-provided position we continue to fulfill our call to tell of God's hope to the nations.

One day I read from Habakkuk 3:10, "The Sovereign Lord is my strength; he makes my feet like the feet of a deer, he enables me to go on the heights." The writer meant it spiritually, but I decided to apply it physically. As I watched my own sons run and play, it occurred to me that rather than allowing a physical handicap to set the limits of my activity, I should strive to set an example for others. If wheelchair-bound athletes can participate in the Special Olympics, then perhaps I could raise the bar, testing the extent to which God's grace might lead, encouraging the world's hurting handicapped along the way. I began running again in order to go beyond the limitations of wearing a prosthetic. From this new endeavor followed the formation of 'Running for Hope,' a non-profit organization that would serve as a bridge for me to share my life experiences with other amputees, land mine and war victims, the handicapped, and anyone else in the midst of struggles who would have a heart to hear the hope I have in Jesus; to know the great joy of sharing in the resurrection life of Jesus that is beyond the pain of daily life. I long for others to hear they can count on God to take them from suffering to healing, from death to life, from one who has felt the same pain of hopelessness. This is the highest mission of Running for Hope.

Running for Hope fits so beautifully with the vision and call to minister to all the nations. Around the world in war ravished lands, thousands are left wounded and maimed through the loss of limbs. Running for Hope uses the opportunity of serving the need for encouragement and physical help as an open door to bring the good news of Jesus to a world of hurting people. By physically helping the poor and disabled in the Middle East, we demonstrate a practical love. It is an opening into the Muslim world that would never allow us to enter as missionaries. Through the ministry of Running for Hope, we are able to stand beside those who have been injured and are looking for help from those who understand their needs. The Muslim world is tired of their hateful killing and revenge. It is looking for the love that wins out against hate. Christ's love is seen when we help them on a practical basis. We can then share with them why we love and have hope from personal experience, presenting to them the gospel of Jesus.

Running for Hope has already collected containers of equipment for the handicapped. These donations have been forwarded to Lebanon for those in need and will be sent also to Africa. We are beginning to develop relationships with churches and clinics in war-torn parts of the world where these gifts can most effectively be used to encourage and rehabilitate the victims of the world's hate and violence. We pray also that this ministry in Jesus' name will give us the opportunity to bring the good news of the King of Kings to nations and peoples who still have never heard.

Each year Running for Hope sponsors a 5K run as a fundraising effort for the ministry. As I train for this event, I hope my example of going beyond my limits is an encouragement to others that we must pray for the endurance and stamina necessary to bring the gospel to the nations, even to our enemies. The apostle Paul often uses the metaphor of the athletic competition as a type of the Christian life and calling. Following his example and exhortation, we continue to strive to fulfill our calling to all the nations of the world. We race to bring the good news of Jesus' kingdom to all, to the Jew, the Muslim, and even the tepid Christian! We continue to reach forward for the victor's crown that Jesus may be all in all. Our hearts and minds are always open to discover the next steps God would have us take in order to be for him a shining star among the nations, holding forth the word of life in Jesus' precious name.

In 2010, Luna and I appeared at the courthouse in Milwaukee, Wisconsin, and took the oath that has made us citizens of the United States of America. The years of difficult adjustments to a new culture have been well worth the effort. We are both grateful and proud to have been received among the many millions who before us have found a safe haven and a land of opportunity in this great melting pot on the North American continent. Like so many others before us, that frightening journey of cultural reorientation was the result of personal spiritual renewal and the quest to worship and serve God freely. More than anything else, it has been our earthly pilgrimage with heaven in mind that lies at the heart of our rejoicing over the privilege and possibilities of our new citizenship here in the world.

Of course we will always hold a certain sense of longing and love for that land which first gave us birth, Lebanon, but in reality, we understand that much of our affection is in fact only a dream, like a faint memory of a time and a place that no longer exists, if ever it did, a Camelot-like desire for the lost, the fanciful, and the impossible. It takes a type of death to self, a bittersweet sting in the soul, to yield such daydream fantasies and replace them with earthly realities. The Lord's providence brought us to our heavenly citizenship through trials in Lebanon, using the missionaries from the United States, as well, who glimpsed their own vision of God's kingdom to the nations and we are grateful. We now see ourselves as being a new generation of missionaries with an expanded vision of that call which will continue until every knee bows and every tongue confesses that Jesus Christ is Lord!

US citizenship 2010

We are grateful for the advantages that our new earthly citizenship provides. The ability to travel and minister throughout the world will be greatly enhanced with a U.S. passport. I pray the nations of the world will be open doors where I can fulfill the calling I first heard so long ago. As

God provides the opportunities, I hope to freely minister the gospel of Jesus Christ in any nation. I have learned from experience God's kingdom transcends earthly allegiances and provides the grace to reconcile all humanity to God and to each other. My international experiences and my role as nations pastor at Eastbrook Church provide a wide open door to reach out in so many ways to the lonely and lost from all around the world.

From the base camp of Eastbrook Church, I see wonderful opportunities to expand and reach out to the nations through the Running for Hope ministry. So many areas of the world have been made hazardous not only by landmines, but also by terrorist and other military actions. Every year thousands of persons are injured, maimed, dismembered, and killed by such tragedies. This wasting of human life and potential affects not only military combatants, but also women, children, and the elderly. I can share from personal experience that there is hope beyond such accidents. My desire is to further the ministry of Running for Hope by providing medical and prosthetic needs, helping put their lives back together. If I can show love and compassion for the hurting, doors may open to show many the way to the greatest healer of all, Jesus Christ.

Another opportunity has come through the Billy Graham Association. I have been invited to be an executive leader for the international church in Milwaukee, and to participate in the planning of the 2011 Rock the Lake event being planned for the metropolitan Milwaukee area. A major effort is to be made to share the wonderful news of Jesus with the numerous international communities in the area. This work fits so closely with the call that God placed on my heart in the early days of my walk with him.

The real challenge to the ultimate international community, which is the church, is the calling to be one people with a common and unified citizenship in the kingdom of God. That citizenship transcends the secular attitude of multi-culturalism and multi-ethnicity which is incapable of rightly dividing between soul and spirit. Lebanon is like all of the other nations of the world in that it has not yet submitted itself to the righteousness that only comes from God through Jesus Christ. It is unique among the nations of the world in that it finds itself positioned on the front lines of another of God's great controversies, his dealings with his ancient people, the natural seed of Abraham. It is this longing for the reconciliation of all of God's children, in Lebanon, Israel, the Muslim nations, and in all of the godless, secularized nations of the earth that Luna and I find the love of our heritage blended together with the desire that all would discover their joy in heavenly citizenship.

The hope for the nations lies only in the peace that Jesus gives. It is not only my native land, Lebanon that continues to suffer the violence of hatred and war. All the nations of the earth stand poised on the edge of destruction as a result of mutual hate. The wars of the Middle East threaten the entire earth with a firestorm of violence. As international leaders seek compromise through treaties, they discover an inability to break through the religious hatreds and ethnic intolerances hindering the most noble of causes. What these world officials and national armies can never accomplish is the healing of the human heart. It is our calling as Christians, as the Church of Jesus Christ, to bring to the nations what secular leaders cannot offer. The world can only seek to enforce peace and harmony through an outward show of force and law. Our calling is to bring to all the nations the love of God through Jesus Christ. He alone can save not only Lebanon, but also the entire family of nations. This is the reality I came to understand. It changed the direction of my life and will be the driving force for me as long as I live.

Postscript

The story and lessons of my life seem to be only in mid-course. God's whole plan for me is not yet completed. Indeed, it would seem that the Lord has barely begun to lay the groundwork in my life as a preparation for the fulfillment of his vision.

It is with gratitude that I confess all of His ways with me have been good. How is it that a believer can look at great tragedies, even the loss of a leg, and lovingly and gladly acknowledge the wisdom of God's ways? It is because the child of God has come to understand that a gracious heavenly Father will go to any lengths to win the heart of his child. And he knows that the material with which he has to work is not always the best. And so it was in my case. A spoiled child of Lebanon with no adequate knowledge of his Lord stumbled into the chaos of the Middle East with the hardness of heart and bitter hatreds of soul that so easily spring up in the unregenerate heart of our Adamic nature. It was only the mercy of God that refused to leave me in that state. He began to speak to me and disciplined me sorely. And his chastening has begun to bear fruit.

My youngest son, Joseph, asked me the other day, "Do you miss your leg?" Of course I miss my leg. His question displays the faith and insight of a child. He has glimpsed the truth that makes each of us special and the unique way God deals with us to lead us into His kingdom and teach us to walk in his ways. The cost may often seem high and the discipline severe. But the pain is always a small price to pay for the unspeakable treasure we gain!

You may recall that I shared earlier about going as a child to the pastures with my shepherd grandfather. There was one sheep very important to him. That sheep was strong and particularly sensitive to the voice of my grandfather. So a bell had been tied around his neck the ringing of which prompted all of the flock to follow him. One sheep, therefore, was very important. He heard the shepherd's voice and followed—and the ringing of the bell caused all the other sheep to follow as well. In ways I sense that to be a parable for my own life. God has led me in a difficult and dangerous way that has made me especially sensitive to know and follow the voice of Jesus, the chief shepherd of the sheep. And he has, so to speak, tied a bell around my neck. It is the testimony of the Holy Spirit in the power of whom I call to all the sheep, "Follow Him!" I feel a responsibility to tell all my story that it should be a witness to the nations to follow Jesus.

And so I wonder what precious fruit may now lie in the future? He has taught me much. He has opened doors of opportunity. He has filled me with the hope of his kingdom that has come. And the overpowering vision has been for the light of Christ to the nations—all nations. I invite you now to pray with me, to labor with me, that we may all be His Good soldiers and shine as stars in the kingdom of our blessed Lord Jesus! The future will be bright.